ROUTLEDGE LIBRARY EDITIONS: LIBRARY AND INFORMATION SCIENCE

Volume 18

COLLECTION MANAGEMENT IN SCI-TECH LIBRARIES

COLLECTION MANAGEMENT IN SCI-TECH LIBRARIES

Edited by
ELLIS MOUNT

LONDON AND NEW YORK

First published in 1989 by The Haworth Press, Inc.

This edition first published in 2020
by Routledge
2 Park Square, Milton Park, Abingdon, Oxon OX14 4RN

and by Routledge
52 Vanderbilt Avenue, New York, NY 10017

Routledge is an imprint of the Taylor & Francis Group, an informa business

© 1989 The Haworth Press, Inc.

All rights reserved. No part of this book may be reprinted or reproduced or utilised in any form or by any electronic, mechanical, or other means, now known or hereafter invented, including photocopying and recording, or in any information storage or retrieval system, without permission in writing from the publishers.

Trademark notice: Product or corporate names may be trademarks or registered trademarks, and are used only for identification and explanation without intent to infringe.

British Library Cataloguing in Publication Data
A catalogue record for this book is available from the British Library

ISBN: 978-0-367-34616-4 (Set)
ISBN: 978-0-429-34352-0 (Set) (ebk)
ISBN: 978-0-367-42437-4 (Volume 18) (hbk)
ISBN: 978-0-367-42445-9 (Volume 18) (pbk)
ISBN: 978-0-367-82414-3 (Volume 18) (ebk)

Publisher's Note
The publisher has gone to great lengths to ensure the quality of this reprint but points out that some imperfections in the original copies may be apparent.

Disclaimer
The publisher has made every effort to trace copyright holders and would welcome correspondence from those they have been unable to trace.

Collection Management in Sci-Tech Libraries

Ellis Mount
Editor

The Haworth Press
New York • London

Collection Management in Sci-Tech Libraries has also been published as *Science & Technology Libraries*, Volume 9, Number 3, Spring 1989.

© 1989 by The Haworth Press, Inc. All rights reserved. No part of this work may be reproduced or utilized in any form or by any means, electronic or mechanical, including photocopying, microfilm and recording, or by any information storage and retrieval system, without permission in writing from the publisher. Printed in the United States of America.

The Haworth Press, Inc., 10 Alice Street, Binghamton, NY 13904-1580
EUROSPAN/Haworth, 3 Henrietta Street, London WC2E 8LU England

Library of Congress Cataloging-in-Publication Data

Collection management in sci-tech libraries / Ellis Mount, editor.
    p. cm.
  "Has also been published as Science & technology libraries, volume 9, number 3, Spring 1989" — T.p. verso.
  Includes bibliographies.
  ISBN 0-86656-933-2
  1. Technical libraries — Collection development. 2. Scientific libraries — Collection development. I. Mount, Ellis.
Z675.T3C59   1989
025.2'1865 — dc19   89-31115
                                                   CIP

Collection Management in Sci-Tech Libraries

CONTENTS

Introduction	**1**
Collection Management in Sci-Tech Libraries:	
An Introduction	**3**
Ellis Mount	
Collection Development Policies	5
Criteria for Selection	8
Selection Tools	11
Making Selections	21
Weeding Collections	21
Costs of Literature	22
Conclusion	23
The Impact of Weeding on Collection Development:	
Sci-Tech Collections vs. General Collections	**25**
Beatrice Kovacs	
Introduction	25
Collection Development and Weeding	28
Tools Available to Aid in Weeding	30
Format Considerations in Weeding	32
Conclusion	33

The Precarious State of Academic Science Library Collections   37
Patricia B. Yocum

Introduction   37
Needs of Academic Scientists   38
Costs of Science Serials   40
Crises in Science Library Budgets   43

Collection Assessment of Biotechnology Literature   47
Kathleen Kehoe
Elida B. Stein

Methodology of Assessment   49
Conclusion   54

Dynamical Systems, Fractals and Chaos: A Guide for the Selector   57
Mary Kay

Introduction   57
Monographic Literature   59

Humanities and Social Sciences Librarians in the Science-Engineering Library: Utilization and Implications for Effective Collection Development and Reference Services   63
Donald G. Frank
Christine Kollen

Introduction   63
Collection Development   64
The Reference Function   67
Formal Orientation and Training   69
Conclusion   70

SCI-TECH COLLECTIONS   73
Tony Stankus, Editor

Information Sources in Surface and Colloid Chemistry   75
Tina Chrzastowski

Introduction   75
Resource Tools   78

Textbooks	79
Monographic Series	81
Conferences	82
Journals	83
Indexes and Abstracts	89
Current Awareness Tools	91
Online Databases	92
Organizations	93

SPECIAL PAPER

Editorial Preparation of the *International Dictionary of Medicine and Biology*   **97**
Sidney I. Landau

Translation Efforts	98
English Language Word List	100
Definitions of Terms	102
Editing Process	105

NEW REFERENCE WORKS IN SCIENCE AND TECHNOLOGY   107
Arleen N. Somerville, Editor

SCI-TECH IN REVIEW   113
Karla Pearce, Editor
Giuliana Lavendel, Associate Editor

SCI-TECH ONLINE   119
Ellen Nagle, Editor

DIALOG Sold to Knight-Ridder	119
ASIS Annual Conference	119
Online '88	120
Database News	121
Search System News	122
Publications and Search Aids	123
Education	124

LETTER TO THE EDITOR   127

Introduction

Building a collection that meets the needs of its users is a very important responsibility. A collection which is inadequate for a given library can prove to be a serious drawback. Building a suitable collection requires planning, careful use of budgets and wise selections on the part of those making choices. There are many obstacles to the process of achieving an appropriate sci-tech collection, not the least of which is the high cost of scientific and technical literature.

This issue covers all aspects of sci-tech collection management. The first paper, by the editor, aims at providing a summary of basic principles and practices involved in the building and weeding of such collections. The second paper, by Beatrice Kovacs, is chiefly concerned with the role of weeding in sci-tech collections, with comparison made to weeding collections outside the sci-tech sector.

In the next paper Patricia Yocum discusses the budgetary dilemma, faced by practically all academic libraries, brought on by the extraordinarily high costs of sci-tech journals. The needs of academic scientists are described in the context of how they affect academic libraries. Two other papers deal with academic collections. The first by Kathleen Kehoe and Elida B. Stein, describes a project carried out at Columbia University that was aimed at assessing the holdings of current monographs on two subspecialties of biotechnology at that school. One result of the project was the determination of the size of the budget needed in these subject areas. The other paper, by Mary Kay, also at Columbia University, describes the development of interest among scientists in dynamical systems, a field of current interest in many fields of science. She lists recommended literature on the subject.

The following paper is by Donald G. Frank and Christine Kollen, who tie in the responsibilities for collection development with those of reference service, specifically discussing these fields in terms of

© 1989 by The Haworth Press, Inc. All rights reserved.

the level of performance that can be expected from librarians in sci-tech libraries who are trained in the humanities or the social sciences.

The collection development paper for this issue is by Tina Chrzastowski; her topic is information sources in surface and colloid chemistry, a topic of continuing interest in many disciplines. The issue's special paper, written by Sidney I. Landau, describes the monumental task of editing the *International Dictionary of Medicine and Biology*.

Our regular features complete the issue.

Ellis Mount
Editor

Collection Management in Sci-Tech Libraries: An Introduction

Ellis Mount

SUMMARY. Provides a summary of the basic aspects of managing a collection of scientific and technical materials. Discusses collection development policy statements, criteria for making selections, examples of published sources listing current publications, making selections and policies for weeding collections. Includes a brief review of costs of sci-tech literature.

The building and care of collections of scientific and technical materials is a responsibility of many types of libraries, whether they be devoted entirely to sci-tech disciplines or need to collect in other major fields as well. Because sci-tech disciplines seem rather arcane to many librarians and information center personnel, it may be worth a review of some of the basic principles that have evolved over the years for building and managing such collections. There is nothing new or startling in this paper; rather, the purpose is to consolidate ideas and concepts that are scattered in many books and

---

Ellis Mount is Research Scholar, School of Library Service, Columbia University, New York, NY 10027. He received the BS (Physics) from Principia College, MS (Physics) from Northwestern University, MS (Library Science) from the University of Illinois, and the DLS from Columbia University.

This paper is based on a presentation made by the author at a meeting sponsored by the New Jersey Library Association, Reference Section, held October 22, 1987, at East Brunswick, NJ. The meeting was entitled "Science and New Jersey: the Future is Here."

Permission to reproduce the example pages was kindly given by the publishers of the publications shown in the figures. Their cooperation is appreciated.

© 1989 by The Haworth Press, Inc. All rights reserved.

4 *COLLECTION MANAGEMENT IN SCI-TECH LIBRARIES*

periodical articles on this subject. The author's experience in this field is also the basis for some of the contents of the paper.

An obvious goal for most libraries is to develop a "good" collection for the subject areas they cover. A few libraries aim at more than a mere "good" collection, but funding usually precludes this choice for most libraries. At any rate, developing a "good" or even a "superior" collection depends upon four basic steps:

1. Development of a suitable collection policy
2. Development of a set of criteria for making selections
3. Development of a number of sources for learning what is available
4. Development of a policy for weeding the collection

In other words, you need a collection development policy so that you know what kind of a collection you're trying to develop; you need a set of criteria for selection to help ensure that you're actually building a collection to match the policy; you need reliable, thorough information on what is actually available for the collection; and you need a policy for weeding the collection to keep it geared to the needs of its users.

Even when these steps are followed, it is not a simple matter to develop a "good" collection. An article that appeared in 1987 pointed out some of the aspects of deciding whether or not a collection was "good."[1] For example, what methods of evaluation should be used — comparing the titles in the collection with comprehensive bibliographies on a given topic, or seeking comments from knowledgeable users, or measuring the number of items sought by library clients that were *not* in the collection, etc.? Another point in the article was that of deciding when an evaluation should be made, in view of the changing nature of many organizations and user populations.

Still another question to be answered has to do with the desirability of including library clients in the team doing the evaluation. A challenge is raised by the authors of the article cited concerning the current practice of assuming that the size of a collection provides a very accurate measure of the worth of a collection. Another question involves the needs of the clients using a particular collection.

What might be good for a medium-sized public library might be inadequate in a university supporting a large research effort. An additional aspect is to evaluate the availability of material from other organizations, such as reliable sources for interlibrary loans or network members with strengths in these subjects. Thus it is seen that development of a suitable collection is *not* a trivial matter. The next section illustrates the variations in depth of interest in particular subject areas.

COLLECTION DEVELOPMENT POLICIES

Returning to the four steps previously named, it is probably rather obvious that a suitable collection development policy must be prepared so it can serve as a guide to those creating the collection. Without a well thought out policy, the collection is apt to grow like the proverbial Topsy. It would be just as foolish for a person to begin a two-week vacation trip without any plan for what should be done during the trip or where one is to go as it would be for a library to have no goals or policies for its collection, be it sci-tech or not. A policy should normally be broad enough to last several years, but it would be a rare library where the policy, once decided upon, needed no further attention or updating during the course of several years; what looked reasonable five years ago might be totally out of date now.

Thus a policy statement should be relatively easy to update, to encourage its revision, yet not be so short as to be trivial. There are at least two formats in which collection development policies could be presented—either written or computerized.

Written Policies

The most common method is written policy statements, using simple prose descriptions of the goals of the collection. They shouldn't be complex nor very detailed, but they should at least serve in some measure to guide selection decisions. A policy statement for an imaginary minimum level general sci-tech collection in a college setting might look something like this:

The XYZ Library will develop a collection for science and technology that will consist of literature on all major topics which are of current interest and which are appropriate for college level students studying these subjects. No effort will be made to collect exhaustively on any particular topic, nor will scholarly works written for the specialist be sought. Current monographs and textbooks should match the courses taught and be of an appropriate level of difficulty. Several periodicals which cover science and technology at the level of students in these courses will be maintained for current years; certain titles of particular interest will be held for at least ten years. A reference collection will include current encyclopedias, dictionaries, handbooks and the like, along with printed indexes and online access to the body of literature covering subject fields being taught. In addition attention should be given to the selection of books and a few periodicals on sci-tech subjects that would appeal to students not majoring in these disciplines. The needs of the faculty for more advanced literature must be balanced against the availability of funds for serving all users. Use should be made of interlibrary loans for filling requests falling outside the normal scope of the collection, but they should not be a substitute for maintaining a collection needed to support the college's program.

This sort of statement would provide some guidance to selection officers, but policy documents of this sort should be shown to appropriate faculty representatives for their recommendations before being adopted. It follows that budgets should be requested that would allow a library to maintain the type of collection called for in a statement. It should be reconsidered and revised every few years, or if major changes are made in the general nature of the college's goals. This example would represent a minimum collection, and many schools would aim higher than this, if funds permitted.

Most libraries do not have the same degree of interest in and need for every subject field in their collections. The larger the library or library system the more likely the range of interest would vary greatly from one topic to another. Large research libraries, such as those typical of the Research Libraries Group (RLG), have over the years adopted a rating system for their collections in which there are six levels, ranging from a topic of no interest to a comprehensive level. A brief summary of the detailed description which appeared in an RLG publication[2] is as follows:

Level	Description
0	*Out of scope*: the subject is not collected.
1	*Minimal level*: a subject area which contains little beyond very basic works.
2	*Basic information level*: consists of current materials that introduce and define a subject but cannot support any advanced courses or research.
3	*Instructional support level*: a collection that is adequate to support undergraduate and most graduate study.
4	*Research level*: a collection that contains the major published source materials as well as material in all pertinent foreign languages. Fully adequate to support research.
5	*Comprehensive level*: a collection that aims at including all significant works of recorded knowledge. The aim is to be exhaustive in scope.

Thus it is clear that collection development statements can have a broad range of scope, depending upon the subject areas and the needs of the users of a particular library.

It should be noted that very specific decisions are not spelled out in the statement; to do so would make an almost unmanageable document, one that would need constant revision as the curriculum changed over the years.

Computerized Policies

An alternative method of creating a guideline for collection development is to prepare it in machine-readable form, readily adapted to updating and revision. This format is better suited to more complicated library collections, such as those in large universities or research libraries, particularly in cases where there are many separate libraries maintained. The likelihood of overlapping responsibilities leads to duplication of effort or, on the contrary, to instances where one library falsely assumes that another library would cover a given topic. Prose statements would become very complex in trying to show overlapping collection areas.

Many libraries have made use of this system in recent years. An article published in 1973 describes the development of such a plan for Columbia University Libraries.[3] The Research Libraries Group has experimented with a computer-based method for determining which RLG member would be responsible for certain subjects and disciplines. Their plans assign one library for each subject area to have the ultimate responsibility for retention of major works.

One feature of such systems is the identification of different levels of collection strengths, using categories such as those described above as developed by RLG. The range of scopes of the collections gives the precision needed to identify the level or strength at which a collection is maintained. Another feature is that of coding the languages in which collections are maintained, such as English, Oriental, European, Middle Eastern, etc. A given collection might be strong in several languages.

In view of the prevalence of the Library of Congress classification system at large libraries, most computerized policies use it rather than the Dewey Decimal system. At any rate, these computerized systems assign a code to each pertinent class, indicating the level of strength maintained. One system even has a dual notation system, indicating both the present strength and the level to be aimed at, if the two are not synonymous.

No matter which method of maintaining a policy for collection development is chosen, the method will be no better than the care given to follow the goals that were identified. A system that is carefully prepared and then forgotten is no better than a system that was never developed.

CRITERIA FOR SELECTION

Having a carefully developed collection development policy is merely the first step towards creating a good collection. Specific criteria for making selections are required. While no two selection officers are apt to make the same selections in a given library, having criteria to guide selections makes it more likely that uniformity would be achieved.

It is clear that making selections on the basis of reviews, advertisements and listings is much harder than making selections on the basis of having seen a particular piece of literature before making a selection. Those libraries having large enough budgets for purchasing new literature have the option of setting up approval plans with cooperating book jobbers or dealers. Having the literature in hand simplifies the following of criteria. Since many libraries, for whatever reason, do not have the advantage of establishing approval plans, the following criteria may be doubly important parts of the selection process. Many of those listed below may seem very obvious, but to newcomers to the selection process all these steps are worth considering:

Monographic Works

1. *Subject matter* — the most attractive, well-written and well-edited book in the world should be ignored if the subject content doesn't match the needs of the library.

2. *Similar holdings* — an otherwise excellent piece of literature might be very similar or even identical in treatment to one or more pieces of literature already in the collection. Then a decision has to be made as to the desirability of adding something that does little to strengthen a collection. Sometimes extra copies of a work are purposely added if its use is heavy.

3. *Cost* — many publications are not selected because their costs are more than the budget will bear. It is usually a sad moment, to have to pass up an otherwise excellent choice because of its cost. In some cases ways can be found to save money in other parts of the budget so as to make selections in spite of costs, but this can be done only a finite number of times before running into budgetary difficulties.

4. *Audience for whom written* — the level of difficulty and the purpose of a book, often discussed in the preface, must be considered so as to avoid selections which are either too elementary or too advanced for the average user. The statements by authors and editors in prefaces must be compared with an examination of the work itself, as the authors may be either very modest in describing the book as being elementary in nature or else very mistaken as to the

10   COLLECTION MANAGEMENT IN SCI-TECH LIBRARIES

degree of difficulty at which the work was written. Some books described by authors as being suitable for undergraduates are in fact understandable only by a small group of experts, while authors with a rather exaggerated opinion of their book have been known to state in the preface that they have prepared comprehensive treatises, yet readers may feel the level of the books are far below that imposing status. Again, this is a factor that can be determined only by direct examination of the work.

5. *Authors or editors* — in some cases the authenticity of a work can be judged by the reputation or the record of the persons responsible for it. Some authors are so consistent in the quality of their writing that a decision could be swayed by that factor alone. It pays to be acquainted with the names of the leading writers in a given field.

6. *Date of information* — in sci-tech subjects it is particularly important to determine if the information is up to date or not, since these disciplines change so much with time. Checking the age of the citations cited in a book is one measure of the currency of information. Some theoretical treatises are not affected as much as works on a more time-dependent topic, such as books listing sources for hardware or software or other types of directories.

7. *Physical factors* — there are several earmarks of a publication with good physical characteristics, such as an attractive print font, a sturdy binding, clear drawings or photographs, etc. In many cases good physical characteristics might be the deciding factor for selecting a publication. In some disciplines, such as biology, the photographs and diagrams are extremely important. This factor is almost impossible to take into consideration unless one sees the book before selecting it, or the rare case where a reviewer happens to comment on these features.

8. *Language in which written* — most users of sci-tech collections in this country do not have much facility with foreign languages, even in academic and research organizations. Therefore one should think twice before buying a monograph written in non-English languages unless there is some assurance it can be read by an appropriate user of the collection.

9. *Other sources* — if a library is part of a network in which interlibrary loans are easily managed, a factor to keep in mind is the

possibility of obtaining a particular book on loan, if it appears to be of marginal interest. It would be a bad decision to plan to borrow publications which are apt to be in heavy demand.

Serials

In choosing periodicals most of the above criteria still apply and some different ones should also be considered.

All of the criteria for monographs seem applicable to serials. However in considering the backgrounds of authors and editors, it is no longer a matter of checking on one or two persons since there are so many writers from issue to issue. However an examination of the credentials of a selection of authors of papers in the journal would give some idea of the status of typical contributors.

Sponsorship—journals which are sponsored by professional organizations sometimes are more highly regarded than journals having a commercial sponsorship. This generalization does not hold for many fine commercial publications, some of which are among the most important serials published.

Indexes/databases in which indexed—because it is so important to be able to locate articles in periodicals quickly, knowing which journals and other serials are indexed and where they are indexed is a key factor in deciding which subscriptions to place. It is just as vital to know which ones are covered by online databases as which ones are included in printed abstracting/indexing services.

SELECTION TOOLS

There are several sources of information about new publications, both monographs and serials. One obvious source is advertisements placed by publishers. They vary greatly in the amount of information furnished—some merely list a title in the midst of an annual catalog, while at the other extreme separate sheets might be issued for a single title, perhaps done in attractive colors and sent to thousands of potential buyers.

Advertisements have the virtue of being timely (sometimes issued far in advance of actual publication, causing those who ordered on the basis of the ad to wonder what delayed their orders).

12 COLLECTION MANAGEMENT IN SCI-TECH LIBRARIES

One of the chief defects of advertisements is that they are biased in favor of the publication — no publisher is going to describe the book as being a poor choice for selection. Even so, there are many books whose subject matter and/or authors are so likely to be worth a purchase that the risk of buying on the basis of an advertisement is very slight. Advertisements also appear in periodicals; the pros and cons of such ads are the same as for individual mailing pieces.

A less risky, but slower, process of selection depends upon waiting for reviews of the books (or new serials) to appear in journals carrying reviews (not all of them do). Reviews appear in many periodicals; each journal has its own policies as to the number of reviews per issue, the type of publication to be reviewed, the length and type of the review and other variations. Some review many books, with short annotations the norm, while others favor a few reviews which provide lengthy descriptions of the books. Some restrict themselves to books written in English, while others seek out foreign language titles to include.

Each selection officer would be well advised to make a definite list of journals to check for reviews since they vary so much as to the subject matter of books, their level of treatment of subjects, their language, their degree of being current, etc.

Some of the major sources of information about current publications are worthy of comment at this point. The following selections are examples of what exists; no attempt is made here to be exhaustive in listing all the sources of this type.

Examples

Annual Publications

Scientific and Technical Books and Serials in Print. New York: Bowker; 1971 — .

> A typical volume of this useful series will contain around 120,000 titles of monographs plus nearly 18,000 serials. The book, a spinoff of the Bowker series, *Books in Print*, provides author, title and subject indexes to monographs, while the serials are listed by subject and title. The serials are international in scope. Besides the usual bibliographic information, costs are included along with addresses of publishers. (See Figure 1.)

Neibauer, Alan. DisplayWrite 2 & 3: A Self-Paced Guide. 256p. 1986. pap. text ed. 16.95 (ISBN 0-8273-2627-0); instr's. guide 10.00 (ISBN 0-8273-2628-9). Delmar.

Schamp, Cathleen L. PC Word Processing with DisplayWrite II & III. LC 85-73533. (Illus.). 220p. 1985. spiral bdg. 15.95 (ISBN 0-942728-25-4). Custom Pub Co.

Schwartz, Linda K. How to Use DisplayWrite 3. Rinehart, Janice S., ed. (Illus.). 88p. 1986. 89.00 (ISBN 0-917792-37-8); quick reference guide & 4 tapes incl. FlipTrack.

Todd, Gail. Displaywrite Three Made Easy. 300p. (Orig.). 1985. pap. 17.95 (ISBN 0-07-881174-0). Osborne-McGraw.

Williford, Jacklyn M. Word Processing with DisplayWrite III. LC 85-22600. 156p. 1986. pap. 16.95 (ISBN 0-471-83070-4). Wiley.

DISPOSAL OF REFUSE
see Refuse and Refuse Disposal
DISSECTION
see also Anatomy, Comparative–Laboratory Manuals; Anatomy, Human–Laboratory Manuals; Zoology–Laboratory Manuals

Bohensky, Fred. Photo Manual & Dissection Guide of the Fetal Pig: With Sheep Heart, Brain, Eye. (Illus.). 1978. 7.95 (ISBN 0-89529-058-8). Avery Pub.

Cuello, A. C., ed. Brain Microdissection Techniques. (IBRO Handbook Ser.: Methods in the Neurosciences). 186p. 1983. 67.95 (ISBN 0-471-10523-6, Pub. by Wiley-Interscience); pap. 34.95 (ISBN 0-471-90019-2, Pub. by Wiley-Interscience). Wiley.

Washington, Allyn J. Basic Technical Mathematics with Calculus, Metric. 4th Metric ed. 1985. text ed. 34.95x (ISBN 0-8053-9545-8); instr's guide 5.95 (ISBN 0-8053-9546-6). Benjamin-Cummings.

Zaidman, S. Almost-Periodic Functions in Abstract Spaces. 144p. 1985. pap. 24.95 (ISBN 0-470-20621-7, Co-Pub. with Longman). Wiley.

Zammuto, A. P. & Mufich, C. J. Drafting Experiences in Metrics. 80p. pap. 6.00 (ISBN 0-87006-241-7). Goodheart.

Zaustinsky, E. M. Spaces with Non-Symmetric Distance. LC 52-42839. (Memoirs: No. 34). 91p. 1978. pap. 10.00 (ISBN 0-8218-1234-3, MEMO-34). Am Math.

DISTANCES–MEASUREMENT
see also Telemeter

Burnside, C. D. Electro-Magnetic Distance Measurement. (Illus.). 128p. 1971. pap. text ed. 12.95x (ISBN 0-8464-0363-3). Beekman Pubs.

Cadogan, Peter H. From Quark to Quasar. (Illus.). 192p. 1985. 24.95 (ISBN 0-521-30135-1). Cambridge U Pr.

Crippen, G. M. Distance Geometry & Conformational Calculations. LC 80-42044. (Chemometrics Research Studies Ser.). 58p. 1981. 49.95 (ISBN 0-471-27991-9, Pub. by Research Studies Pr). Wiley.

Digby, John. The Structure of Bifocal Distance. 1974. sewn in wrappers 3.95 (ISBN 0-685-78874-1, Pub. by Anvil Pr). Small Pr Dist.

Moriya, T., ed. Electron Correlation & Magnetism in Narrow Band Systems. (Springer-Series in

Van Winkle, Matthew. Distillation. (Chemical Engineering Ser.). 1967. text ed. 52.00 (ISBN 0-07-067195-8). McGraw.

DISTILLATION, DESTRUCTIVE
see also Coal Gasification; Coal-Tar Products; Cracking Process; Mineral Oils; Oils and Fats; Petroleum

Rose, L. M. Distillation Design in Practice. (Computer-Aided Chemical Engineering Ser.: No. 1). 308p. 1985. 65.00 (ISBN 0-444-42477-6); pap. 29.75 (ISBN 0-444-42481-4). Elsevier.

DISTILLATION, FRACTIONAL
see also Distillation, Molecular

Butzer, et al, eds. Approximation Theory & Functional Analysis: Anniversary Volume. (International Series of Numerical Math: Vol. 65). 632p. 1984. text ed. 48.95x (ISBN 3-76431-574-1). Birkhauser.

Plate Distillation Columns. 20p. 1962. pap. 9.00 (ISBN 0-8169-0026-4, E-10). Am Inst Chem Eng.

DISTILLATION, MOLECULAR

Hollo, J., et al, eds. Applications of Molecular Distillation. 210p. cancelled (ISBN 0-685-27534-5). Adlers Foreign Bks.

DISTILLING INDUSTRIES

Breslin, W. R. Solar Still. 36p. 1979. write for info (ISBN 0-86619-030-9). Vols Tech Asst.

Downard, William L. Dictionary of the History of the American Brewing & Distilling Industries. LC 79-6826. (Illus.). xxv, 268p. 1980. lib. bdg. 55.00 (ISBN 0-313-21330-5, DOD/). Greenwood.

Shanken, Marvin R. The Impact American Distilled Spirits Market Review & Forecast.

FIGURE 1. *Scientific and Technical Books and Serials in Print*

14   COLLECTION MANAGEMENT IN SCI-TECH LIBRARIES

Science and Technology: a Purchase Guide for Branch and Public Libraries. Pittsburgh: Carnegie Library of Pittsburgh; 1960—.
> This consists of an annotated list of new sci-tech books of general interest that were received by the Carnegie Library during the year. The 1987 issue contained more than 1,000 titles. Books are entered by title, arranged by their Library of Congress classification. There is an author index, which also contains titles when no author is given. Annotations are quite brief but appear to be adequate. (See Figure 2.)

Best sci-tech books of 19—: an annotated selection of the 100 best titles of last year for general collections. Compiled by Ellis Mount and Barbara A. List. *Library Journal.*
> An annual feature, usually in the March 1 issue, it consists of 100 books considered by the compilers as being the best publications of the year for general collections. Entries are arranged by main entry under broad categories such as Physics, Biology or Technology. Each item is annotated. Selections are geared to titles which would appeal to public library collections, particularly those of interest to the lay reader. (See Figure 3.)

More Frequent Publications

New reference works in science and technology. *Science & Technology Libraries*. New York: The Haworth Press, Inc.; 1980—; v.1—Quarterly.
> A regular feature of this journal is a section devoted to reviews of sci-tech reference books, such as handbooks, dictionaries, directories, etc. Each item is annotated, and all disciplines of science and technology are included. Essentially limited to English language works. (See Figure 4.)

New Technical Books: a Selective List with Descriptive Annotations. New York: New York Public Library, The Research Libraries; 1915—. Bimonthly.
> A selective listing of English language books, with emphasis on the pure and applied physical sciences, mathematics, engineering, industrial technology and related disciplines. Level of difficulty of selected items ranges from college level to very specialized monographs and conference proceedings. Each

TC HYDRAULIC ENGINEERING

Goldsmith, Edward
Social and environmental effects of large dams. Sierra Club Bks., 1986. 404p. index. $29.95. 85-2235.
A compelling case against large-scale water projects.

Woollett, William
Hoover Dam: drawings, etchings, lithographs, 1931-1933. Hennessey & Ingalls, 1986. 133p. index. illus. $14.95. 86-289.
Graphic chronicle of the construction of Hoover Dam.

Caiati, Carl
Real-life scenic techniques for model railroaders. Tab Bks., 1987. 161p. index. bibliog. illus. (some color) $14.95 pap. 86-6000.
Step-by-step instructions in creating realistic effects from commercially available materials.

Carlson, Pierce
Toy trains: a history. Harper & Row, 1986. 160p. index. bibliog. glossary. illus. (some color) $24.95. 86-45084.
Covers from 1840-1955. With price guide.

FIGURE 2. *Science & Technology: A Purchase Guide*

Space Studies

BOND, Peter R. **Heroes in Space: from Gagarin to** *Challenger*. Basil Blackwell. 480p. ISBN 0-631-15349-7. $24.95.
The accomplishments and disappointments of the 100 or so manned space flights from the United States and the Soviet Union are chronicled in this well-written book. Emphasis is on the flight crews as each mission is described. Should have a wide appeal.

COOPER, Henry S.F., Jr. **Before Lift-Off: the Making of a Space Shuttle Crew.** Johns Hopkins. 270p. ISBN 0-8018-3524-0. $18.50.
A fascinating portrayal of the life of astronauts being trained for a mission in 1984, by a writer for *The New Yorker*. The complicated tasks to learn, the comradeship that develops among team members, and the dangers faced by the crews are all made vivid by Cooper. The tragic *Challenger* accident is discussed, as are the exhilarating moments of successful missions.

DAVIS, Joel. **Flyby: the Interplanetary Odyssey of** *Voyager 2*. Atheneum. 256p. ISBN 0-689-11657-8. $17.95.

FLORMAN, Samuel C. **The Civilized Engineer.** Thomas Dunne Bks: St. Martin's. 258p. ISBN 0-312-00114-2. $15.95.
Another welcome book by the author of *The Existential Pleasures of Engineering*. In this volume he once again shows his talent as he discusses the real nature of engineering and engineers through such topics as: engineering education, idealism in engineering, conflicts between engineers and nontechnical executives, the role of women in engineering, and the causes of disasters such as the *Challenger* accident. This book is a must.

RAINS, Darell L. **Major Home Appliances: a Common Sense Repair Manual.** TAB. 160p. ISBN 0-8306-0747-1. $21.95; pap. ISBN 0-8306-2747-2. $14.95.
Clearly shows how broken applicances can be repaired at home by application of procedures explained and illustrated for the do-it-yourselfer. The copious supply of photographs adds to the clarity of the explanations of repairing dishwashers, washers, dryers, refrigerators, etc.

Weapons

BONDS, Ray, ed. **The Modern US War Machine: an Encyclopedia of American Military Equipment and Strategy.** Crown. 248p. ISBN 0-517-56097-6. pap. $14.95.
A study of equipment and policies governing military activities of the United States, based on the contributions of 14 specialists in the field. The first portion of the book is devoted to a discussion of the military/intelligence services and their policies. The second half offers detailed descriptions of military, naval, and airborne weapons. A well-organized and thorough book.

GAY, William & Michael Pearson. **The Nuclear Arms Race.** American Lib. Assn. (Last Quarter Century, No. 1). 270p. bibliog. ISBN 0-8389-0467-X. pap. $29.95.
A comprehensive look at nuclear weapons, including historical aspects, current problems, and outlook for the future. The book serves as a reference book on the subject and was written to appeal to the adult and young person wanting a serious discussion of a critical topic. For all collections on nuclear warfare and its prevention.

FIGURE 3. *Library Journal: Best Sci-Tech Books*

PHYSICAL SCIENCES

Copper, silver, gold and zinc, cadmium, mercury oxides and hydroxides. Edited by T. P. Dirkse, New York: Pergamon; 1986. 360p. $100.00. ISBN 0-08-032497-5. (Solubility data series. Vol. 23.)

This reference work presents and evaluates data for the oxides and hydroxides of two groups of transition series metals from Groups I and II of the Periodic Table. Literature sources include *Chemical Abstracts* 1907-1984, Gmelin, *Handbuch der Anorganischen Chemie* prior to 1907, and the work of Mellor. However, with few exceptions, no works published before 1900 were used for preparing the 342 data sheets. Indexes include ones for the system, registry number, and authors. For all serious chemistry collections in industry and academe. (RGK)

Data for biochemical research. 3d ed. Edited by Rex M. C. Dawson and others. New York: Oxford University Press; 1986. 580p. $59.00. ISBN 0-19-855358-7.

A rather general collection of data on compounds required by the average biochemist. (Carefully complete so to avoid materials needed only by specialists in individual areas.) Thus the work is concise enough (over 4,000 compounds) for laboratory use. Arrangement is essentially by chemical categories (e.g., phosphate esters excluding nucleotides and coenzymes; steroids; pharmacologically active compounds). For collections on biological chemistry. (RGK)

Handbook of glass properties. By Narottam P. Bamsal and R. H. Doremus, New York: Academic; 1986. 680p. $135.00. ISBN 0-12-078140-9.

This is a collection of critically selected and correlated data on silicate glasses, but commercial glasses from European and Japanese manufacturers, nonsilicate glasses, for example, have been slighted. Scores of tables and figures of the most recent data are include: there is very strong bibliographic support. For reference collections in most science and technology libraries in industry and academe. (RGK)

FIGURE 4. Science & Technology Libraries: New Reference Works

item is annotated. Entries are arranged by Dewey classes; there is an author index. (See Figure 5.)

SciTech Book News: an Annotated Bibliography of New Books in Science, Technology and Medicine. Portland, OR: SciTech Book News; 1976(?) — . Monthly.

A listing of selected books in the physical and biological sciences, mathematics, medicine, engineering, technology and

520 Astronomy

Ghosh, Sanjib Kumar
1133 Analytical photogrammetry
2nd edition. NY: Pergamon, 1988. 308p $45
526.9′82 TR693 87-29134 ISBN 0-08-036103-X

Contents: Instrumentation. Coordinate systems. Geometry of photographs. Refinement of photo coordinates. Object-photo relationship. Design of projects. Multiple-photo applications. Self-calibration and constraints. Unconventional cases. Index.

Note: Analytical photogrammetry is being applied in numerous fields other than the conventional fields of mapping — such as architecture, biology, medicine, and industry. The main purpose of the book is to establish aspects of analytical photogrammetric concepts and procedures. Intended for graduate students, researchers, and practitioners in photogrammetry and remote sensing. Focuses on certain new data-reduction techniques and various analytical instruments in the field. (RA)

Harrison, Edward Robert
1134 Darkness at night: a riddle of the universe
Cambridge: Harvard U Pr, 1987. 293p $25
520′.9 QB28 86-32701 ISBN 0-674-19270-2

Contents: The riddle begins. The riddle develops. The riddle continues. Appendixes. Index.

Note: Beginning with ideas about space and the universe developed by scholarly divines of the Middle Ages, theoretical approaches through time to the dark night-sky riddle are discussed. The Aristotelian, Epicurean, Stoic, Cartesian and Newtonian systems of thought are covered, along with more modern theories which evolved with the discovery of galaxies, the new astronomy and modern cosmology. Appendices containing historical documents, notes on the text, a good bibliography and an index complete the text. For institutions having an interest in astronomical history. (LAF)

FIGURE 5. *New Technical Books*

agriculture. Emphasis is on graduate level texts, scholarly treatises and professional references. Almost all entries are annotated. Entries are arranged by Library of Congress classification. (See Figure 6.) Beginning in 1988 some 1500 entries from this publication will be included in Bowker's CD-ROM product *Books in Print with Book Reviews PLUS*.

Technical Book Review Index. Pittsburgh: JAAD Publishing Company; 1935-1988. (Ceased publication.)
For many years this index presented a selection of book reviews of sci-tech books, often useful in case a selection officer had overlooked a title when it was first published. It is listed because its demise was quite recent, and librarians who were familiar with it may have wondered why it wasn't included.

Other Sources

In a brief introduction such as this it is not possible to list all the sources of current materials needed for sci-tech libraries. For example, technical reports and government documents are listed in publications other than those listed above. In order to provide some guidance to readers new to those formats, the following indexes are traditional tools for keeping abreast of new materials of this sort.

Monthly Catalog of U.S. Government Publications. Washington: Government Printing Office; 1895 — . Monthly.
A useful publication for listing of new documents, but emphasis is on Congressional publications and non-technical agencies. Some exceptions are documents on agriculture, the environment, geology and mining. Most of the sci-tech documents are listed in other indexes, such as the next index listed.

Government Reports Announcements and Index. Springfield, VA: National Technical Information Service; 1946 — . Semimonthly.
An extremely useful index, including citations for thousands of technical reports supported by federal funding, covering all areas of science and technology. All items are annotated; most are available in either full size or on microfiche. Has indexes in each issue as well as annual indexes by subject, author,

20   *COLLECTION MANAGEMENT IN SCI-TECH LIBRARIES*

LANGUAGE

P98   87-35649   0-387-96691-9
Natural language generation systems.
Title main entry. Ed. by David D. McDonald and Leonard Bolc (Symbolic computation. Artificial intelligence)
Springer-Verlag, ©1988   388 p. $37.00
Topics covered in this volume include discourse theory, mechanical translation, deliberate writing, and revision. Chapters contain details of grammatical treatments and processing seldom reported on outside of full length monographs. Produced from variously typed manuscripts.

SCIENCE (GENERAL)

Q101   87-28986   0-12-289510-X
Mathematics applied to science; in memoriam Edward D. Conway.
Title main entry. Ed. by Jerome Goldstein et al.
Academic Pr., ©1987   309 p. $34.50
E.D. Conway was, for two decades preceding his death in 1985, an admired and influential member of the mathematics faculty at Tulane University. He contributed importantly to the applications-base theory of (partial) differential equations. The present memorial volume contains two biographical sketches and thirteen technical articles (by P. Lax, J. Smoller, others) reflective of Conway's professional preoccupations. Neatly typed, carefully produced. (NW)

Q127   87-94593   0-8020-6606-2
Inventing Canada; early Victorian science and the idea of a transcontinental nation.
Zeller, Suzanne
U. of Toronto Pr., ©1987   356 p. $15.95 (pa)
Cloth edition, $35.00.

Q127   87-34010   0-8014-9496-6
The launching of modern American science, 1846-1876.
Bruce, Robert V.
Cornell U. Pr., ©1988   446 p. $12.95 (pa)
A paper reprint of the 1987 edition.

FIGURE 6. *Sci-Tech Book News*

agency, report number and contract number. Also available on-line as the database NTIS. A standing order for microfiche on given subjects can be placed, thus simplifying the acquisition of reports, with cost savings over ordering individual reports.

MAKING SELECTIONS

The tools listed in the previous section provide a multitude of titles from which to select. A large part of the building of a collection is knowing what is available, but making good selections is often a matter of practice, or trial and error.

One important feature of collection development is to give proper heed to requests from library users. Many of them can provide excellent titles worth acquiring; other users never think of suggesting or requesting purchases. One pitfall to avoid is that of purchasing everything each library user suggests. Each person probably has a personal interest in a given topic, so if each requested item is purchased it is easily possible to develop a collection that overemphasizes certain special topics. A good balance must be maintained among the various subjects making up the collection. One must not be afraid to turn down requests, even from strong library supporters, if the collection is getting too many items on a few pet topics of requestors.

WEEDING COLLECTIONS

The process of removing literature from a collection, often called weeding, is one that is important to most libraries if for no other reason than to create space for newer materials. However the weeding of sci-tech collections may cause more apprehension among librarians than working with literature outside the sci-tech fields. The better one's knowledge of the subject matter to be weeded, the less tension there would be. Much has been written about weeding in general, but the paper in this issue by Kovacs,[4] which covers applications to sci-tech collections, is recommended.

One step in weeding collections of any sort that provides a bit of

COLLECTION MANAGEMENT IN SCI-TECH LIBRARIES

insurance that no permanent damage might be unintentionally done is simply to ask a few library clients who are knowledgeable about the subjects being weeded to look over items earmarked for removal. While this is no guarantee that every library user would agree with the final group of items to be weeded, at least it is almost certain that no valuable items, including old classic works whose age might deceive a neophyte librarian, would be removed from the collection. Since it is very embarrassing to be told that an important book was weeded, and since it can be time-consuming and expensive to find a replacement in such cases, one rule of thumb for the librarian new at the process might be: When in doubt, keep it! This at least saves loss of important material. As one gains more experience, skill in weeding can be developed.

COSTS OF LITERATURE

It would be foolish to gloss over the budgetary difficulties of most sci-tech libraries in the past few years. The main problem is the continuing increase in sci-tech serials. For many years science and technology have been the most expensive subjects for literature, particularly for periodicals; recent years have seen even larger annual increases. Both foreign and domestic titles are affected, although the current exchange rate for European currencies has made their periodicals even more expensive, with any number of journals costing over $2,000 per year. Certain American indexing services have for several years cost more than $5,000 per year.

A recent periodical article attempted to give librarians some workable method of evaluating different journals, such as counting the number of articles from a given periodical that were cited by writers in the field.[5] The article listed some of the causes for subscription price increases and possible solutions. Many sci-tech libraries have had no alternative but to cut back on monographs in order to keep major subscriptions to journals intact. It is not a happy situation.

CONCLUSION

It is hoped this brief introduction to the important process of managing sci-tech collections will prove to be of some value to those getting involved for the first time. It is a process that continued effort in doing will lead eventually to real skills.

NOTES

1. Futas, Elizabeth; Vidor, David L. What constitutes a "good" collection? *Library Journal*. 112(7): 45-47; 1987 April 15.

2. *RLG collection development manual*. 2d ed. Stanford, CA: Research Libraries Group, Inc.; 1981; p. 2-1 to 2-2.

3. Yavarkovsky, J.; Mount, E.; Kordish, H. Computer-based collection development statements for a university library. *ASIS Proceedings*. 10: 240-241; 1973.

4. Kovacs, Beatrice. The impact of weeding on collection development: sci-tech collection vs. general collections. *Science & Technology Libraries*. 9(3): 25-36; 1989 Spring.

5. Barschall, Henry H. The cost-effectiveness of physics journals. *Physics Today*. 41(7): 56-59; 1988 July.

The Impact of Weeding
on Collection Development:
Sci-Tech Collections
vs. General Collections

Beatrice Kovacs

SUMMARY. What impact does the removal of materials have on the decision-making for collection development? The literature of librarianship indicates that weeding should have a major impact, but practice does not appear to follow theory, according to responses from 31 selectors interviewed in research on collection development. Is there a difference between weeding sci-tech collections and general collections? Again, the answer appears to be no. This article reviews the literature of weeding and summarizes the weeding practices of some selectors in sci-tech, academic, and public libraries. Some differences between sci-tech and general collections are discussed.

INTRODUCTION

A great deal has been written in the past few years about collection evaluation and the identification of materials that are no longer determined to be of value in the provision of service to the library's clientele. In looking at the literature of librarianship, some questions arise concerning the elimination of materials from the collections. Two of the questions are addressed in this article. They are: What impact does the removal of materials have on the decision-

---

Beatrice Kovacs received a DLS from Columbia University School of Library Service, an MLS from Rutgers University, and is currently Assistant Professor in the Department of Library and Information Studies at the University of North Carolina at Greensboro, Greensboro, NC 27412-5001.

© 1989 by The Haworth Press, Inc. All rights reserved.   *25*

26   COLLECTION MANAGEMENT IN SCI-TECH LIBRARIES

making for collection development? Is there a difference between weeding sci-tech collections and general collections such as those located in academic or public libraries?

Once again, as seems true throughout library literature, authors appear to be discontented with descriptive names used by others. Therefore, a number of words and phrases are now in use to define the phenomenon of removing materials from collections: weeding, pruning, deaccessioning, discarding, retirement, deselection, reverse selection, negative selection, disposal, and storage. For the purposes of this paper, the term "weeding" will be used as an arbitrary synonym for all the aspects of removal of all materials from the active collection.

There are a number of articles written about weeding academic library collections,[3,4,5,7,13,15,19,20,23,26,31,35,39,42,43,44,46,47] and about weeding public library collections.[1,2,10,27,29,33,34] Some of these articles refer to weeding sci-tech materials, within the context of more general collections.

The author of a recent text on collection development said, "Weeding materials [in special libraries] is easier because of the comparatively straight-forward and predictable use patterns, the homogeneous nature of the clientele and its small size, and the relatively narrow goals of the special library."[14,p.294] However, special librarians have authored a number of articles discussing the difficulties and problems with eliminating materials from the collections.[12,17,18,21,36,38]

The difficulties of weeding types of materials are reviewed in many of the articles. For example, weeding and discontinuing serials are frequent topics,[3,4,5,7,8,11,18,24,36,38,40,41,46,48] as well as weeding reference[13,34,46] and rare book collections,[44] and managing media[47] and microcomputer software[10] collections. Methodologies for conducting weeding programs are described, including overlap studies[31,32] and bibliometric and citation analyses.[3,4,6,7,8,20,23,24,25,32,38,40,48]

Considerations for the disposal of materials are also offered, including storage,[12,23,43] auction[30,42] and book sale.[1] A cost model for storage and weeding is offered.[23] There are reports of surveys of weeding practice in public libraries[27] and academic libraries,[13] as well as a survey of weeding policies in medical libraries.[17]

Are there really those "straight-forward and predictable use patterns" which make weeding the collections easier in the type of special library which specializes in sci-tech materials? Are all the concerns in the literature not as relevant in weeding sci-tech collections? The answer to both questions is "probably no." It is difficult to take an absolute stand on the issue because sci-tech collections are similar only in the subject matter contained in the materials. There are so many varieties of sci-tech collections that sweeping generalizations would be inappropriate. One needs to specify which "type" of library in which the collection is housed before one is able to give a definitive answer. Corporate, society, academic, public, and other sci-tech libraries all have special needs, diverse clientele, and unique services.

As one author states, "Weeding is one of the most sensitive issues facing librarians today. Why then is this process so highly recommended in theory and so rigorously ignored or avoided in practice?"[43,p.47] Slote[37,p.20-22] identifies factors discouraging weeding: emphasis on numbers of materials in collections as criteria of quality; lack of time to perform required tasks in the weeding process due to other work pressures; "emotional and intellectual blocks" to removing materials from the collections ("sacredness"); and "hard-to-apply and sometimes conflicting criteria." Much of the literature in recent years has addressed the need for weeding with suggestions concerning the ways in which to overcome some of these issues.

Some authors offer methodologies which have the potential to create objective criteria to aid in identifying materials to be weeded. These include bibliometrics and citation analyses, serials rationalization studies, user surveys, and circulation and use studies. In sci-tech collections, another objective methodology deals with the age of the material under the assumption that anything older than "x" years is no longer accurate/vital/current/important/useful to the collections. When any or all of these methodologies are employed, the authors still acknowledge that there are always exceptions.

The two most commonly identified reasons for weeding collections are lack of space (for monographic and non-print materials) and lack of budget (for commitment to serials, continuation of subscriptions, and binding or other processing costs). It seems that practical necessity, rather than theoretical reasoning, is the impetus for weeding in most libraries.

How is the weeding process for sci-tech collections different from the weeding process for general collections? The resistance to weeding seems to be similar for all types of collections. There is the reluctance to eliminate materials which have been, and have the potential to continue to be, useful. There is the acknowledgement that the time needed to perform thoughtful and informed weeding cannot be found in the workday, especially in understaffed libraries. The reasons *for* weeding, in practice, seem to be similar, namely lack of space and lack of budget. The weeding process, both in theory and in practice, seems to be the same for all types of libraries.

COLLECTION DEVELOPMENT AND WEEDING

The differences between general collections of materials and collections of sci-tech materials are not always obvious. Certainly the need for accuracy and currency is apparent for most collections, but for many sci-tech collections the recency of information is paramount, although there are sci-tech collections for which historical materials are extremely valuable. Sci-tech collections are often expected to contain only authoritative and reliable materials on one or more specific branches of the sciences and/or technology, while general collections are expected to contain a "balance" of points of view on almost any issue a patron may wish to pursue.

Does weeding and/or the weeding process have an effect on the collection development decision-making for sci-tech collections? Is there a difference in the effect of weeding between sci-tech collections and general collections?

This author conducted a series of studies on decision-making in collection development over the past six years. These studies, as yet unpublished, designed to identify the thought processes of practicing selectors, were undertaken in public, academic, and special libraries. Thirty-one selectors were interviewed for periods of six to twelve weeks and asked to recall what they were thinking when they made collection development decisions during the previous week.

Regarding the subject of weeding, the selectors were asked to identify what materials they weeded from the collection during the previous week. They were also asked what impact this weeding had on their collection development and selection decisions. In most cases, when weeding occurred it involved discarding superceded editions of monographs (particularly reference books) and withdrawal of records for items declared missing or lost. Damaged materials no longer deemed usable because of poor condition were also discarded. Occasionally, in both sci-tech and academic collections, short runs of discontinued or inappropriate serials were weeded and offered to other libraries, primarily to provide additional shelf space for new materials.

The selectors indicated that any weeding that occurred had little impact on their decision-making for selection and collection development. In a few instances, selectors indicated that as a result of having to discard a book in bad condition, they had to search for replacements which would address the same subjects. Most of the weeding occurred as a result of collection development decisions rather than having impact on those decisions. In other words, materials were weeded because an earlier decision to purchase items caused the present materials to no longer be relevant to the collections. Superceded editions and older monographs about rapidly changing fields of science or technology were removed. Duplicate copies in overcrowded stacks were removed to make way for new materials purchased for the collections.

None of the libraries had formal collection evaluation and/or weeding programs, although many had policy statements on procedures for weeding the collections and for disposal of unwanted items. Lack of staff and lack of time were reasons common to all the libraries in these studies for not conducting regular, or even intermittent, collection evaluations. The librarians all subscribed to the philosophy that collection evaluation is important and informed weeding is essential to the usefulness and relevance of the collection for the clientele. Almost all of the selectors said something similar to: "One of these days, we will have the time and, hopefully, the staff to do it right. Meanwhile. . . ."

If the problems concerning weeding are so similar in these libraries, then is there a difference between sci-tech libraries and aca-

30   COLLECTION MANAGEMENT IN SCI-TECH LIBRARIES

demic or public libraries regarding the process of weeding? Regarding the process, the answer is no. However, librarians have some tools for developing sci-tech collections that are sometimes overlooked as tools for weeding too.

TOOLS AVAILABLE TO AID IN WEEDING

Many sci-tech librarians are aware of, and have used, the *Journal Citation Reports* of the Institute for Scientific Information (ISI) as indicators of the "importance" of journals and the ranking of locally held journals in scientific disciplines. A number of articles have been written about uses for citation analysis for collection evaluation.[3,6,7,8,24,32,38,40,48] Often, rankings have been used to justify the addition of journal titles to the holdings of libraries. The rankings can be used as one criteria to eliminate titles from holdings, also. For example, locally held titles from which there are fewer articles cited in the literature than titles covering similar subjects could be considered for cancellation. The rationale for this is the assumption that if fewer articles in a journal are cited by authors, there is the likelihood that there is less quality or substantive information published in that journal. Caution should be taken in using journal ranking as the only criteria for cancellation. Other factors to be considered, in conjunction with the citation studies, include: Is the journal too new to be included in many of the indexing and abstracting sources commonly available to researchers? Does the journal publish only a few carefully refereed articles each year in a narrow discipline? Is this a journal in which researchers in the local institution publish works? Is this a journal that is heavily used by the clientele of the library? If the answer to any of these questions is "yes," then careful consideration should be given to continuing the subscription.

There are some tools which have been used by selectors for years to identify materials to purchase for collections, which in their new electronic formats can be helpful in weeding also. One particular product, which has exciting possibilities for aiding the weeding process, is *Books In Print With Book Reviews Plus* by Bowker. The print version of this source often contains materials considered too old by selectors who are looking for the most current material available. The CD-ROM version, however, is updated quarterly. It contains new books published or available in the American book market with full bibliographic information and sources for book reviews, as well as the reviews themselves (reviews in two major science journals have recently been added). Of particular usefulness is the searcher's ability to access the data by subject, with Boolean logic. Librarians can target older books in the collections as candidates for weeding and determine if there are any authoritative newer books as replacements which would cover the subject, or new editions which supercede the material held.

"Best books" lists can be used as tools for weeding also. Subject areas which seem to have excessive numbers of books, causing a concern for lack of balance or over-coverage in the collections, can be evaluated through the use of lists of highly regarded books created by experts in their fields. Some of these lists are created periodically by professional associations or organizations. Care must be taken, however, when using these lists to evaluate the appropriateness of the collections. It should be remembered that the lists were created by individuals who might have their own prejudices for inclusion or exclusion of books and other materials. It should also be remembered that the collections might look perfect if the same lists used to evaluate them were the lists used to create them.

With the advent of OCLC, microcomputers and the myriad of programs available for statistical and other analyses, new methodologies have been created to target material for weeding. Data manipulation in overlap studies can identify subject areas in which duplication is held in a library system, region, consortium, or cooperative.[31,32] While this information has often been gathered to provide a basis for cooperative collection development, it includes valuable data for weeding collections. Mutually held material which may be of occasional value to the clientele could be considered as candidates for weeding, if accessible through interlibrary loan. Here, too, there needs to be caution. Clear agreements should be made by participating libraries that the last copy of a work should be retained, and therefore be available in the region.

Online catalog query and circulation use studies can aid in determining both subject areas which are not of interest to the clientele and titles of materials never requested or circulated. Careful use of

32 COLLECTION MANAGEMENT IN SCI-TECH LIBRARIES

these data, combined with other information-gathering methods, can aid in informed weeding of materials. Since many of the resources discussed here are automated, use of them is less time-consuming than methods used in the past.

FORMAT CONSIDERATIONS IN WEEDING

Print formats have received almost all the attention in the literature of weeding. Most of the methods of data-gathering for identification of materials to weed that have been discussed here are appropriate for print materials only (monographic and serial publications). Even Slote's excellent and comprehensive work on weeding[37] discusses only print materials. Sci-tech and general collections now have increasing non-print components, and weeding methodologies should be addressed for these materials also. For many general and sci-tech collections, video, audio, and computer file formats are purchased, used, and stored.

Selectors interviewed during the study period did not weed any media from their collections. They felt no need to do so because there was plenty of room for storage. Perhaps it is too soon for most libraries to be facing the problem of overcrowding in their media collections, but the time will come. Criteria for weeding these materials, tested and revised, should be developed before a crisis of overcrowding develops. Ongoing evaluation of the non-print collections should be occurring before the task becomes too large.

An interesting article presenting general ideas and specific suggestions for the creation of media collection development programs in academic libraries was written by Whichard.[47] His suggestions and comments might be an excellent foundation for the creation of sci-tech media collection development programs. Selection of public access microcomputer software was discussed by Dewey[10] and could also be adaptable for sci-tech collections. Little else appears in the literature at present, including any mention of weeding non-print materials in collection development texts.[9,14,16,22] It is still unclear what criteria will need to be considered with the new technologies, such as CD-ROM, until more is known and published than is now available.[28,45]

CONCLUSION

Weeding is a process that, in theory, is vital to the maintenance of an active, useful collection in any type of library. It is expected that evaluating the collection, in order to determine what to purchase, will also identify materials to be weeded and that the weeding would be done. It might also be expected that the weeding process would have an effect on the future purchases of materials for the collections, identifying areas in which new materials should be bought. It appears, however, that in practice weeding does not occur for the reasons stated in theory, and weeding seldom has any effect on decision-making for selection.

Every selection or purchase decision carries with it a calculated risk that the item will not meet the needs of the library's clientele. When material in the collection is identified as not appropriate for the library, it should be eliminated. Weeding should be based on something more than the need for shelf space; it should be an integral part of a collection development program. Libraries should have collection development and management programs that include weeding as a major function of selectors. At present, this does not seem to be the practice in the libraries studied; and, there seems to be no difference between weeding practice for the sci-tech collections and for the general collections. The impact of weeding seems the same for all the collections. All librarians need to rethink their views on weeding, and initiate active weeding programs if they have not already done so. Find the time for weeding; it is well worth it!

NOTES

1. Battistella, Maureen S. A cooperative medical library/public library book sale: new avenue for marketing the academic health sciences library. *Bulletin of the Medical Library Association*. 73(3): 283-285; 1985 July.

2. Beckerman, Edwin. Housing library collections. *Collection Building*. 8(3): 29-30; 1986.

3. Bensman, Stephen J. Journal collection management as a cumulative advantage process. *College & Research Libraries*. 46(1): 13-29; 1985 January.

4. Bostic, Mary J. Serials deselection. *The Serials Librarian*. 9(3): 85-101; 1985 Spring.

5. Bousfield, Wendy. Boundary spanners and serials deselection. *The Serials Librarian*. 10(3): 23-31; 1986 Spring.

34 COLLECTION MANAGEMENT IN SCI-TECH LIBRARIES

6. Boyce, Bert R.; Pollens, Janet Sue. Citation-based impact measures and the Bradfordian selection criteria. *Collection Management*. 4(3): 29-36; 1982 Fall.

7. Broadus, Robert N. A proposed method of eliminating titles from periodical subscription lists. *College & Research Libraries*. 46(1): 30-35; 1985 January.

8. Broadus, Robert N. On citations, uses, and informed guesswork: a response to Line. *College & Research Libraries*. 46(1): 38-39; 1985 January.

9. Curley, Arthur; Broderick, Dorothy. *Building library collections*. 6th ed. Metuchen, NJ: Scarecrow; 1985: Chapter 14.

10. Dewey, Patrick R. Public access microcomputer software selection. *Illinois Libraries*. 68(6): 369-371; 1986 June.

11. Diodato, Virgil P. Original language, non-English journals: weeding them and holding them. *Science & Technology Libraries*. 6(3): 55-67, 1986 Spring.

12. Eakin, Dottie. Health science library materials: collection development. *In*: Darling, Louise, ed. *Handbook of medical library practice*. 4th ed. Chicago: Medical Library Assoc.; 1983: p. 27-91.

13. Engeldinger, Eugene A. Weeding of academic library reference collections: a survey of current practice. *RQ*. 25(3): 366-371; 1986 Spring.

14. Evans, G. Edward. *Developing library and information center collections*. Littleton, CO: Libraries Unlimited; 1987: Chapter 14.

15. Fisher, William H. Weeding the academic business/economics collection. *Behavioral & Social Sciences Librarian*. 4(2/3): 29-37; 1984/85 Winter/Spring.

16. Gardner, Richard K. *Library collections: their origin, selection, and development*. New York: McGraw-Hill; 1981: Chapter 10.

17. Goldstein, Cynthia H. A study of weeding policies in eleven TALON resource libraries. *Bulletin of the Medical Library Association*. 69(3): 311-316; 1981 July.

18. Grefsheim, Suzanne; Bader, Shelley; Meredith, Pamela. User involvement in journal de-selection. *Collection Management*. 5(1/2): 43-52; 1983 Spring/Summer.

19. Harnly, Caroline D.; Hall, Cynthia; Covert-Vail, Lucinda. Weeding: one answer to an unreasonable problem. *Technicalities*. 5(5): 3-7; 1985 May.

20. Hodowanec, George V. Literature obsolescence, dispersion, and collection development. *College & Research Libraries*. 44(6): 421-443; 1983 November.

21. Hulser, Richard P. Weeding in a corporate library as part of a collection maintenance program. *Science & Technology Libraries*. 6(3): 1-9; 1986 Spring.

22. Katz, William A. *Collection development: the selection of materials for libraries*. New York: Holt, Rinehart and Winston; 1980: Chapter 4.

23. Lawrence, Gary S. A cost model for storage and weeding programs. *College & Research Libraries*. 42(2): 139-147; 1981 March.

24. Line, Maurice B. Use of citation data for periodicals control in libraries: a response to Broadus. *College & Research Libraries*. 46(1): 36-37; 1985 January.

25. Losee, Robert M. A decision theoretic model of materials selection for acquisition. *Library Quarterly*. 57(3): 269-283; 1987 July.

26. Lucker, Jay K.; Herzog, Kate S.; Owens, Sydney J. Weeding collections in an academic library system: Massachusetts Institute of Technology. *Science & Technology Libraries*. 6(3): 11-23; 1986 Spring.

27. Mahoney, Kay. Weeding the small library collection. *Connecticut Libraries*. 24: 45-47; 1982 Spring.

28. Miller, David C. *Special report: publishers, libraries & CD-ROM: implications of digital optical printing*. [s.l.]: DCM Assoc.; 1987.

29. Miller, J. Wesley. Throwing out belles lettres with the bathwater. *American Libraries*. 15(6): 384-385; 1984 June.

30. Model, Peter. Books at auction: the art of deaccessioning. *Wilson Library Bulletin*. 56(1): 33-38; 1981 September.

31. Moore, Barbara; Miller, Tamara J.; Tolliver, Don L. Title overlap: a study of duplication in the University of Wisconsin System Libraries. *College & Research Libraries*. 43(1): 14-21; 1982 January.

32. Mosher, Paul H. Quality and library collections: new directions in research and practice in collection evaluation. *Advances in Librarianship*. 13: 211-238; 1984.

33. Neill, Desmond. Defending duplicates: the value of variant copies. *Wilson Library Bulletin*. 56(9): 669-672; 1982 May.

34. Nichols, Margaret Irby. Weeding the reference collection. *Texas Library Journal*. 62: 204-206; 1986 Winter.

35. Reed-Scott, Jutta. Implementation and evaluation of a weeding program. *Collection Management*. 7(2): 59-67; 1985 Summer.

36. Segal, Judith A. Journal deselection: a literature review and an application. *Science & Technology Libraries*. 6(3): 25-42; 1986 Spring.

37. Slote, Stanley J. *Weeding library collections—II*. 2nd rev. ed. Littleton, CO: Libraries Unlimited; 1982.

38. Smith, Thomas E. The *Journal Citation Reports* as a deselection tool. *Bulletin of the Medical Library Association*. 73(4): 387-389; 1985 October.

39. Stam, David H. "Prove all things: hold fast that which is good": deaccessioning and research libraries. *College & Research Libraries*. 43(1): 5-13; 1982 January.

40. Stankus, Tony; Rice, Barbara. Handle with care: use and citation data for science journal management. *Collection Management*. 4(1/2): 95-110; 1982 Spring/Summer.

41. Stankus, Tony. Journal weeding in relation to declining faculty member publishing. *Science & Technology Libraries*. 6(3); 43-53; 1986 Spring.

42. Streit, Samuel. Research library deaccessioning: practical considerations. *Wilson Library Bulletin*. 56(9): 658-662; 1982 May.

43. Stueart, Robert D. Weeding of library materials—politics and policies. *Collection Management*. 7(2): 47-58; 1985 Summer.

44. Traister, Daniel. Goodbye to all that: a case study in deaccessioning. *Wilson Library Bulletin*. 56(9): 663-668, 1982 May.

45. Urbanski, Verna. Resources & technical services news: CD-ROM takes

center stage. *Library Resources & Technical Services*. 32(1): 12-16; 1988 January.

46. Westbrook, Lynn. Weeding reference serials. *The Serials Librarian*. 10(4): 81-100; 1986 Summer.

47. Whichard, Mitchell. Collection development and nonprint materials in academic libraries. *Library Trends*. 34(1): 37-53; 1985 Summer.

48. Wiberley, Stephen E., Jr. Journal rankings from citation studies: a comparison of national and local data from social work. *Library Quarterly*. 52(4): 348-359; 1982 October.

The Precarious State
of Academic Science Library Collections

Patricia B. Yocum

SUMMARY. The rich diversity of university library collections may also be a source of tension, particularly when the need for substantial, incremental resources recur in one sector. Coupled with pressures to support current research, budget constraints may be converting many academic science libraries into working collections. Addressing the challenges requires understanding the nature of contemporary science and the critical role academic science libraries play in it.

INTRODUCTION

Large research universities pride themselves on the diversity of intellectual inquiry their multiple schools, colleges and departments pursue. And rightly so. American universities have assembled impressive concentrations of human and material resources to promote the advancement of knowledge and its transmittal to current and future generations. The university library, of course, plays a fundamental role in this endeavor. But even while it may be accurate to speak of the library as one entity, it would be misleading to assume that it is a homogeneous enterprise. Like its parent institution—the university—the library must be diverse if it is to support the breadth of research and teaching the university undertakes. Indeed, it is the pluralism of university libraries which makes for the riches they offer and contributes to the centrality they hold in the scholarly community.

Patricia B. Yocum earned a BA (English Literature) at SUNY-Binghamton, an MA (English Literature) and an AMLS at the University of Michigan. Since 1977 she has been Head of the Natural Science Libraries at the University of Michigan, Ann Arbor, MI 48109-1048.

© 1989 by The Haworth Press, Inc. All rights reserved.

Pluralism, though, can also be a source of tension. The very differences which make for diversity impose a demand to be understood differently. They may require different kinds of concurrent organizational views, efforts, policies and practices. Stress may mount when pluralism's constituent parts vary in size, tradition and needs. If the variations persist over a long period of time, tension may become institutionalized and individualized. It can rise especially when the need for additional, often substantial, resources present themselves. Though particular instances may be resolved, the residual impact may be to highlight the underlying differences, leading to disharmony and further tension.

Academic science libraries in big research universities often find themselves as figures in this tension. Too large to be ignored, too central to be dismissed, these libraries are yet too different to fit smoothly into library norms molded largely by the humanities and social sciences. More importantly, their rapidly changing and escalating needs in the area of collection development over the last twenty years have put science libraries in a category of "critical issues" for which there is no quick, easy or certain resolution.

Nor will the problems go away if we wait long enough or hold fast to our present course. On the contrary, the current pressures and growing needs of collection development/information access in academic science libraries have the potential to exacerbate tensions and lead to serious conflict. Because such conflict can be detrimental to a wide range of activities, it is in the common interest to take stock of the situation in order to meet the challenges rationally and dispassionately.

NEEDS OF ACADEMIC SCIENTISTS

To start, we need to look at the community of science. Far from homogeneous, basic science incorporates a rich panoply of fields and subfields. Consider just a few: astronomy, chemistry, and geology; cellular biology, high energy physics, and vertebrate anatomy. Moreover, because basic science is dynamic, new specializations, such as bio-inorganic chemistry and plant molecular genetics, are continually establishing themselves as fields build upon their previous discoveries, intersect with other fields and borrow methods and ideas from each other. Science builds on the past and regularly refers to it. Some areas, such as systematics, work as closely with older material as they do with new. The bulk of modern science concentrates on problems in their contemporary state and, through discovery, shapes the future status of those problems. To appreciate this concentration consider the following analogy. Were this same concentration to apply to the humanities, we would see most historians focusing their scholarship on current events, rather than past ones, thereby molding what happens in the world tomorrow.

Like other disciplines in the liberal arts, basic science is not ipso facto an applied discipline but rather is concerned with answering fundamental questions. For basic science the fundamental goal is to understand how the natural world works. In the last several decades, and markedly in the last ten or fifteen years, opportunities to advance that understanding have accelerated greatly as new, powerful and sophisticated instrumentation has been developed and become the laboratory norm. Capable of super-sensitive, complex measurements not otherwise feasible, modern scientific instruments are costly to acquire. For example, in hiring new assistant professors, it is not uncommon for universities to spend $50,000 to $500,000 for "start up costs" (i.e., expenses for the purchase of equipment and retrofitting of space to house it). Moving a full professor from one university to another costs even more, e.g., over $1 million in some specializations.[1] At the same time, attention must be paid to the equipment needs of established faculty if their research is to remain current.

These needs are addressed in a variety of ways. Academic scientists commonly pool their requests and share equipment among groups and sometimes between institutions. They include the cost of new equipment in their research grants and apply for special "instrumentation" grants. In some cases the grants involve cost sharing whereby the university and the grantor each agree to pay a portion of the expense. In the past private corporations have underwritten costs or donated superceded equipment from their own laboratories. Gifts from private donors and foundations have also helped.

As welcome as it is, though, this assistance does not obviate the fiscal impact on the university. Contemporary science is expensive

40   COLLECTION MANAGEMENT IN SCI-TECH LIBRARIES

and has become so in a relatively short period of time. Spectrophotometers, DNA synthesizers and scanning electron microscopes cost orders of magnitude more than do bunsen burners and petri dishes. Research universities which want to remain on the "cutting edge," or move into that position even in just a few areas, have little choice but to put a greater portion of their funds into basic science than they did just ten or twenty years ago.

COSTS OF SCIENCE SERIALS

Developments in science have implications on the scientific literature and its cost and funding. Superior instrumentation, among other things to be sure, allows for experiments which are more detailed, complex and highly refined. Results, written up as published papers, reflect this situation. Loaded with formulae, symbols, graphs, high resolution photographs et al., current articles are labor-intensive to produce. They often require top-of-the-line production equipment and material to replicate graphics adequately to validate the research they are reporting. In many scientific areas, the characteristics of contemporary published papers contrast sharply with those of a just a few generations ago. Biology offers one of the most pronounced comparisons. A cursory examination of journals from the early 1960s reveals texts dominated by words, sentences and paragraphs complemented by modest illustrations. Except for the content, they suggest strong kinship to publications in the humanities and social sciences. Publications of the 1980s are distinctly different.

Yet librarians, as well as others, often persist in viewing the published products of all scholarship as part of the same genre and subject to similar expectations. This is especially true with respect to costs. As prices rise and budgets tighten, the first line of analysis often is to establish price categories with implied standards of acceptability, for example, $200 as the upper limit. Subscriptions costing below the standard tend to be viewed as less problematic, while titles costing above the standard are targeted for scrutiny and possible cancellation. In times of budget urgency there is logic in this approach. The library which must cut its expenditures by 3%, 5%, or 15% because of a projected shortfall in revenues rarely has sufficient resources to evaluate purchasing commitments in great detail. Decision-making takes time. When faced with a deadline, as well as a targeted dollar amount to cut, librarians are pressed to make as few decisions as possible. Cutting one $500 subscription involves making only one decision; cutting ten $50 titles requires substantially more.

While cost categories may help a library get through a particular fiscal crisis, in their current form and as permanent instruments in budget allocation and collection development they are seriously flawed and sometimes detrimental. Focusing on price, they tend to obscure questions of quality, centrality and value. They may minimize the importance of relationships within the collection which make it richer than the sum of its individual pieces. As suggested above, cost catagories may also overlook differences in production expenses. More importantly, by adopting, even informally, a specific dollar figure as a standard for all disciplines, they ignore fundamental changes that have occurred in scholarship and may heighten tensions in the scholarly community.

The issue of duplicate subscriptions, especially during a budget crisis, can similarly exacerbate tensions. In the past "duplicate subscription" usually connoted two or more subscriptions held by a single library unit. Typically, such titles were used by the clientele in different ways or were used so heavily that one subscription, designated the "binding copy," was acquired as a preservation measure to assure future accessibility. Currently, "duplicate" generally connotes two subscriptions maintained within the university library system, regardless of where the physical pieces are housed. Often these locales are distant from one another i.e., blocks or even miles apart.

It is indicative that talk of cutting duplicates comes reluctantly from science librarians. One can rest assured that the reason is not egocentrism. From experience and out of need, science librarians are sensitive to budgetary constraints. If cancelling duplicates were an easy choice, they would welcome the option warmly. Nor are faculty noted for adherence to collection size as the best measure of quality or importance. Rather, the difficulty in cancelling duplicates, as well as the need to have them in the first place, lies in their centrality to research efforts.

To appreciate this tie we again need to look at the community of science. Although popularized notions would have us visualize the "mad" scientist working alone in his isolated lab, they are far from authentic. On the contrary, to pursue their research, contemporary scientists find it essential to be part of far-reaching communities built upon common interest in solving problems deemed important. Such problems are generally complex, highly refined and may take ten, twenty or more years to solve. The aggregated effort they require lies beyond the capacities of a single person or single research group. There is no individual ownership of a problem or universal "master plan" for solution. Progress is made incrementally, with advancements contributed by and subsequently credited to the researchers who first produce and publish them. Whether corroborating or disproving earlier hypotheses, or offering new theoretical models, experimental methods or analytical techniques, the newest research findings help shape the next questions to be asked and the next experiments to be tried.

In this regime keeping current with others' research findings is vital. For the researcher, keeping current is a continuous, demanding, time-consuming process involving formal and informal channels of communication. Among these, the journal article serves as the public record and the means for providing wide dissemination. Because scientific investigation moves rapidly, ready access to the literature is critical. Access is often by known item (i.e., a specific paper), which is essential to researchers when they are preparing or running experiments, writing or refereeing papers, and preparing grant proposals. But browsing is also important in furthering scientific inquiry. Allowing for the unexpected, browsing can foster fresh perspectives and synthesis of seemingly unconnected notions. Challenging habits of thought, it allows intuition to come into play in the formulation of new ideas. It can be and is done with new literature as well as with old.

Centrality and fast, efficient use of the literature prevails throughout scientific fields. When research specialization is concentrated in a compact locale, a single library subscription to a title may be adequate. But large research universities sprawl and often support similar scientific inquiry in several locations. For example, biological research can be done concurrently in the liberal arts college and the medical or agricultural school. Chemical research can be conducted in a basic science department as well as in the engineering college. In addition, though specializations may differ in perspective or thrust, they often include the same journal titles in the core of their communications networks. In these instances the need for two or more subscriptions to a title becomes compelling. Proposals to reduce the number of subscriptions to one for the entire campus can compromise and even threaten the research process as it is conducted locally.

CRISES IN SCIENCE LIBRARY BUDGETS

Fiscal crises in library budgets are real and can be severe. Those of the mid-1980s are illustrative, though not unique. Confronted by a sharply weakened U.S. dollar and by steep price increases for material, libraries found their budgets insufficient to meet expenditures. Unless financial relief were forthcoming, wholesale reductions in commitments, and journal subscriptions in particular, were inevitable. In some universities, where substantial funds were added to the library budget, the number of titles subsequently cancelled was modest. In other instances cuts were sweeping, topping $100,000. Cancelling serials titles, especially under pressure, is one of the most demanding responsibilities academic librarians exercise. Its bright side includes the chance to clear out the "deadwood," that is, to retire titles whose quality has diminished. Unfortunately, reviewing serials commitments in the 1980s has afforded limited opportunity for this bright side to show in the academic science library. Because large-scale cancellations of serials have been a recurring phenomenon since the early 1970s, librarians often find little "deadwood" left to excise.

More commonly, during the 1980s, the operating definition of "essential title" has been narrowed and the thrust of the science collection concurrently refocused. For many academic science librarians, the core questions have become tortuous. Which faculty members are using which titles in their current research? Can these be retained? If not, to what extent should each kind of research be supported? Whose research should be supported more, whose less? Which titles, if owned, would help faculty win research grants, thereby bringing more money into the university and, through overhead return, possibly to the library? Which research is in least jeopardy if access to material depends on cross-campus transmittal or interlibrary borrowing? Conversely, which titles are not being used by current faculty or their graduate students? If research interests or academic programs have changed, what is the likelihood they will some day be revived? And what claim do new titles have on funds with or without a budget crisis?

In tandem the answers to these questions are marking significant alterations in the character of many academic science libraries. At bottom many of these libraries are moving rapidly away from being comprehensive collections covering the breadth and depth of science and toward becoming special libraries tightly tied to present local research efforts. Their collections are increasingly dominated by English-language publications as foreign language titles fail to meet adequately the tests of current local use or claim on scarce funds. While there is some comfort in noting that English is the principal language of science, it must also be noted that important work (in chemistry and geology, for example) is still being published in other languages. Removing ready access to foreign publications invites American research in affected fields to lose speed and become parochial.

But language is not the only change occurring in collections. Longevity is also affected. Without current faculty research activity, the fact that a library has a strong collection in a subfield provides no assurance that it will continue to develop that collection. Similarly, holding a complete set of a title is no longer sufficient reason by itself to justify a subscription, even if the title dates back to the 19th century and the library is one of few in the country with such holdings. Esoterica, those unusual titles in small print runs which enrich the research collection, is also vulnerable as the library's buying power diminishes.

Changes such as those noted above are happening not by design but by default. They are the product of hard choices driven by pressures of finance, policy and contemporary research. Not all academic science libraries are experiencing the changes to the same degree. On the contrary, some are able to continue building their collections comprehensively. But in an increasing number of in-

stances science librarians are sharing the same painful story of reduced collecting scope and are circulating strikingly similar lists of
cancelled subscriptions. In addition, they are doing this at a time of
increasing scientific productivity and publishing output. In severe
cases, libraries converting to working collections may even fall
short of the new objective and be unable to fill all the demands
current local research places upon them.

The potential ramifications of these developments are serious.
Within the university library they may be leading to creation of a
two-tiered system: the traditionally comprehensive collection in the
humanities and social sciences, and the lesser one in the basic sciences. User and institutional expectations, however, may continue
to presume that collections are consistently supporting research
over a broad spectrum. Discoveries to the contrary can lead to com-
plaints and pressure for additional resources.

The impact on scientific inquiry may be even more severe. Cancelling subscriptions or capping the number of subscriptions a library holds may balance the current library budget, but it also risks
disrupting the scientific research process. On the local level, researchers may need to invest more time in maintaining their communications networks and more effort in accessing vital information. Research may be more difficult to perform and not as "cutting
edge" as it needs to be. Grant proposals may be more difficult to
prepare and of lessened quality, resulting in fewer awards and low-
ered income to the institution.

The greatest risk, though, may be on the national level. For several decades American scientific research has been remarkably productive and the world leader in many fields. Much of this research,
of course, has been conducted by faculty members, graduate students and post-doctoral scholars at universities across the country.
To no small degree, that research has been made possible by the
existence of strong collections in academic science libraries.
Change in the collection strength of a particular library may have
localized effect. But changes occurring in a number of libraries can
have an aggregated impact, disrupting the flow of scientific information and jeopardizing the national research effort.

Nor are near-term prospects sanguine. Costs for library materials
are likely to continue rising. More significantly, they will be joined

by additional expenses for electronic access to information. Already powerful, electronic access will become more so, allowing for bibliographic and textual manipulations not previously possible. Some forms of electronic access, of course, will supplant print versions. Others, however, will not, and the 1990s are likely to see the need for both print and electronic media. Further, because electronic access is expensive and has the capacity to charge fees for each use, information costs are likely to rise substantially. It may well be that the budgetary problems libraries have been facing for the last twenty years are only a prelude to harsher ones coming in the next decade.

Academic science libraries in America have a long, distinguished history of supporting scientific inquiry by providing broad, reliable, community access to the scientific literature. Through their collections, they represent a substantial investment of money, commitment and effort on the part of innumerable individuals and organizations. In the aggregate they constitute a national treasure as well as a national resource in the advancement of science. Their capacity to continue functioning in these roles should be a matter of wide-ranging interest both within and outside universities.

NOTE

1. Blum, Debra E. Cost of recruiting researchers soars as equipment becomes more sophisticated and competition grows. *Chronicle of Higher Education*. 35(6): A18; 1988 Oct. 5.

Collection Assessment
of Biotechnology Literature

Kathleen Kehoe
Elida B. Stein

SUMMARY. An assessment of the current monographic literature of two subspecialties of biotechnology was undertaken in the Science division of the Columbia University Libraries. The two aspects were biocatalysis (an area of interest to chemists, biologists, and engineers) and applied molecular biology, specifically cloning and cell culture (also of interest to chemists, biologists, and engineers). Bibliographies were compiled from holdings of major research libraries, CIP records and publishers' flyers. One of the objects of the assessment was to fill in the gaps in our collection, which is dispersed in 3 libraries. Another object was to develop an understanding of the subject itself, and a third was to document the need for additional funds and analyze the expenditure increases for five years.

Science reference librarians in special and academic departmental libraries are frequently the bibliographers for the libraries they serve. As such, the development of the existing collection is their responsibility. Given the enormous growth rate of science literature in the last two decades, it is no longer a simple matter to keep abreast of the current literature in any of the disciplines.

Librarians are continually making their own informal assessments. An increase in interlibrary loans for certain areas of litera-

---

Kathleen Kehoe is Biology, Physics and Astronomy Reference/Collection Development Librarian for the Columbia University Libraries. She received her BA from Hunter College and the MLS from Columbia University. Elida B. Stein is Chemistry Reference/Collection Development Librarian and bibliographer for chemical engineering at the Columbia University Libraries. She received her BA from Hunter College and the MLS from Columbia University.

© 1989 by The Haworth Press, Inc. All rights reserved. *47*

ture or increasing requests for books and/or journals in a specialty, will often stimulate recognition that the buying in an area is insufficient. The informal approach to reviewing the collection—looking it over and talking to a few knowledgeable patrons, is no longer a sufficient means of assessing the relative degree of literature coverage that has been achieved in a given collection.

A formal collection assessment will provide an objective and accurate picture of a collection's strengths and weaknesses vis à vis the "universe of literature" existing in a particular discipline. Although a formal collection assessment is a time-consuming endeavor, the effort can generate information which is invaluable in the following ways: (1) to help determine the degree to which the collection meets the patrons' needs; (2) to project the costs of adequate acquisitions for sub-disciplines; (3) to help formulate plans for the directions in which the collections will develop in the future; (4) to quantify resources that need to be allocated to new areas of research interest.

Collection assessments are particularly useful in libraries buying in several specialty areas. Academic science librarians who buy for a single discipline, may actually have half a dozen (or more) areas of literature which need to be covered. These days, as most of us do not have a budgetary carte blanche, we are rarely able to collect comprehensively for our disciplines. The situation is further complicated by the increasing numbers of interdisciplinary areas of study whereby researchers' needs may involve the use of several departmental collections. This is true at Columbia, where there are separate subject collections.

In 1987 the Director of Resources of the Columbia University Libraries "inspired" us to do our first formal collection assessments, and we decided that English language monographs in biotechnology would be an excellent area of the literature for us to review. The chemistry and biology librarians were responsible for buying the biotechnology literature, and each of us had noticed the increasing importance of biotechnology. There were external signs of this change, such as the new Elsevier catalog for biotechnology; *Chemical Abstracts* now has a separate tutorial disk on biotechnology for its online system; *Science* and *Nature* now issue yearly guides to products and instruments for biotechnology. This field is of increasing importance to researchers in chemistry, biology and chemical engineering.

"Biotechnology is not a single discipline but rather is a selective amalgam of ideas and techniques of many fields, particularly biochemistry, microbiology, genetics and in some of its most dramatic manifestations, embryology" (Goldsby, 1985). Biotechnology is a relatively new term, but in chemistry the manipulation of organisms to yield products is old — Pasteur's work in fermentation is a celebrated example. This area of work, formerly called industrial microbiology or process biochemistry, is now a part of biotechnology. What is new is an expansion of applied or industrial biology and a revolution in its methodology, which has transformed many traditional high pressure and high temperature processes into enzymatic processes operated with low energy consumption. Enzymes are the catalysts of processes in living organisms — thus they are called "biocatalysts." The use of these processes, as a methodology, is referred to as "biocatalysis." The literature of biocatalysis was chosen to be assessed, as it is the most relevant part of the biotechnology literature for the chemistry and chemical engineering departments.

In the biological sciences the past five years have seen enormous growth in biotechnology research. The explosion is a result of the progress in recombinant DNA techniques. Cloning and the use of cell cultures are two of the central methodologies of biotechnology research. These techniques are utilized in medicine, pharmacology, agriculture, microbiology, genetics and bioengineering. A substantial body of monographic literature in this area has developed in the past five years, and continues growing.

METHODOLOGY OF ASSESSMENT

In order to assess our biotechnology collections we needed very current bibliographies. Existing bibliographies were compiled in 1983 or earlier. The last five years' literature was of critical interest. Therefore a current bibliography had to be compiled for biocatalysis, cloning and for cell cultures.

In chemistry, where there were a limited number of titles and relatively few subject heading and keywords, a list of five years of

50 COLLECTION MANAGEMENT IN SCI-TECH LIBRARIES

literature on biocatalysis was compiled. In biology the constraints of time dictated limiting the list to three years. The methodology for compiling the bibliographies was the same. First, appropriate LC subject headings were searched in RLIN, then keywords were searched in RLIN. Next publishers' flyers for the current year were searched for titles that might not already have RLIN records. Finally, publishers' advertisements in current issues of *Science*, *BioScience*, *Bio/Technology*, *Nature* and *Bio/Techniques* were reviewed.

The subject headings and title words used to search the chemistry literature in RLIN were:

> enzymes — industrial, applications
> immobilized enzymes
> immobilized cells
> immobilized proteins
> biocatalyst, biocatalysts, biocatalysis

The search was limited to a publication date of 1982 or later.

The subject headings and title words used to search for the biology subset were:

> industrial microbiology
> biotechnology
> recombinant DNA
> genetic engineering
> clone, clones and cloning
> cell culture, cell cultures

We were aware that we were limiting our searches to just the holdings of the Research Libraries Group. Unfortunately, at the time the assessment was done, we had no access to OCLC.

Duplicates of titles in the lists were eliminated. The RLIN printouts generated Columbia records with locations for the titles that we owned, which saved searching for call numbers and library locations. The titles were sorted in "books owned" and "books not owned." "Books not owned" were searched in the order file. In some cases the books were already on order. These were treated as "books owned." We then searched the shelves for the "books owned." The "books not owned" list was reviewed to identify titles that should be added to the collection.

We wanted to determine the degree to which the library coverage of our topics is being met and also how much money, if any, we would need to back order any desired material. We also wanted to project how much money we would need to support this growing field for an unknown increased number of researchers.

We met with faculty members who teach courses in biotechnology, who do research in the field and/or who have students doing projects in these areas to discuss their work and their literature needs. They reviewed our lists of "books not owned" and made suggestions.

Until the current assessment neither the chemistry/chemical engineering bibliographer nor the biology bibliographer was buying this literature systematically. We were buying books we believed would be useful to specific investigators or books that had been requested by specific investigators and their groups. The chemistry bibliographer has been buying this literature for approximately five years. The biology department has recently become very active in biotechnology research and in 1986 the biology bibliographer began to buy more titles as a response to new courses and to increased research in cloning and cell cultures.

The chemical engineering material (i.e., biocatalysis) is housed mainly in the engineering library and used mainly by chemical engineers. The cloning and cell culture materials are used by bioengineering researchers, biologists and some biochemists from the Health Sciences campus. Most of these books are shelved in the biology library. Some of these titles are of interest to biochemists and geneticists at Health Sciences and some are duplicate holdings. (See Tables 1 and 2.)

The Science Division libraries owned 58% of the titles generated by the bibliographies we produced. Ten (10) percent of the titles were not owned and of no interest — either because they were dissertations or because they were overly specialized treatments of the subjects. Thirty-two (32) percent of the titles were books we did not own that should be added to the collections.

In order to project the cost of the 43 titles (32%) that we wish to buy, a mean price was generated from the list of the books already

TABLE 1. Availability of Materials

	Cloning and Cell Cultures		Biocatalysis	
	# of items	% of Collection Owned	# of items	% of Collection Owned
1. Not in collection	31		25	
2. In circulation	12	19.4	3	17.6
3. On shelf	27	43.5	10	58.8
4. Reserve	6	9.7	0	
5. Reference	5	8.1	0	
6. New book shelf	4	6.4	0	
7. In process	1	1.6	1	5.9
8. On order	6	9.7	0	
9. On shelf, 2nd search	0		1	5.9
10. Can't locate, 2nd search	1	1.6	2	11.8
TOTALS	93	100%	42	100%

TABLE 2. Science Division Expenditures for Biotechnology Monographs

	BIOCATALYSIS SUBSET		CLONING & PLANT/ANIMAL CELL CULTURE SUBSET	
Year	Amount Spent	# Items	Amount Spent	# Items
1983	$247.00	4	*	*
1984	$256.00	3	*	*
1985	$245.00	3	$742.00	16
1986	$124.50	2	$1,400.00	20
1987	$348.00	5	$2,080.00	26
Total: (5 yrs)	$1,220.50		Total: (3 yrs)	$4,222.00

*
 Data Not Available

COLLECTION MANAGEMENT IN SCI-TECH LIBRARIES

owned. That mean was $82. For the 43 titles we wished to purchase, the cost would be approximately $3,600.

Neither the chemical engineering nor the biology budgets permit us to buy all these titles immediately as the current allocations cannot accommodate such an expenditure for two small specialized areas of the literature.

CONCLUSION

The results of our assessment gave us a clear picture of our holdings. Sixty-six (66) percent of the available imprints were in the biology library or were on order. In the chemistry and chemical engineering subset only 40% of the available titles had been bought. However, only 14 unbought titles (representing 10% of the whole) were suitable for purchase.

Considering the results of the assessment raises several questions. Why weren't the lacking volumes bought at the time of their publication? Since we purchase the bulk of our acquisitions through an approval plan, it seems that these volumes were not offered to us by the vendor. We compared the list of publishers covered by the vendor with the publishers of the titles we were lacking. A small number of volumes were missed because two publishers weren't represented. The balance of the volumes should have been offered on approval and were not. We firm order many volumes that we do not receive on approval but in this case we failed to uncover these titles for firm ordering. This can be attributed to the fact that we were not systematically tracking new biotechnology titles. We will now have to routinely search for new titles in these areas in order to improve our future coverage.

Another question that we must now answer is how we will pay the cost of increased coverage of this literature. The number of books offered each year is growing and the books' costs are also growing. If we spent $2,400 in 1987 it is reasonable to predict that we will need more than that amount in each following year. The 1987 biology acquisitions cost 148% of the 1986 acquisitions. That is likely to recur if we are more successful at identifying titles and if the costs continue to rise. It is our opinion that at least $4,000 per year should be devoted to supporting biotechnology.

There are two possible solutions to this financial problem — request a budget increase to cover the costs or cut down on the acquisitions in some other sub-specialty. Quantifying the current costs of our limited biotechnology coverage clarifies the question as to whether we can broaden our acquisitions in biotechnology to include other areas of the literature such as applied microbiology materials. Obviously we cannot afford to try to cover an additional area of the literature given our current budgets.

Our literature survey was limited to English language monographs. When we interviewed faculty about their needs for this literature, they brought up another issue. They mentioned the need to keep abreast of new serials in this area. One of our patrons had even prepared a list for us! Thus we have another assessment task set up for us — evaluating our serials coverage in biotechnology.

This project was surprisingly labor intensive, and it took the better part of the academic year to complete it. It was a fruitful endeavor. We learned something about the subject of biotechnology and its literature and about a useful tool for evaluating the coverage of specialized areas of literature in our libraries.

Dynamical Systems, Fractals and Chaos: A Guide for the Selector

Mary Kay

SUMMARY. Describes the development of interest among scientists in the subjects of dynamical systems, fractal geometry and chaos, particularly the work of Benoit Mandelbrot and Mitchell Feigenbaum. Following that there is a list of recommended literature, divided into the three groupings of popular treatments, textbooks and surveys, and monographs. The selections constitute important titles on dynamical systems from the mathematician's point of view.

INTRODUCTION

All librarians who are currently working with mathematicians, computer scientists of physical scientists are aware of the high demand for material on dynamical systems, fractal geometry and chaos. Less commonly understood are the close interconnections of these topics. In act, they have in common the study of the phenomenon of nonlinearity.

Benoit Mandelbrot and Mitchell Feigenbaum were the two pioneers of this field, Mandelbrot from the pictorial point of view and Feigenbaum from the mathematical. The two points of view have proved to supplement each other, providing sufficiently convincing material to capture the interest of mathematicians. Since these ideas appear to be useful for modelling complex physical and biological phenomena, interest in the ideas and their application is wide-

---

Mary Kay is Head, Reference/Collection Development, Science Division, Columbia University Libraries, New York, NY 10027. She also acts as Mathematics Library bibliographer and reference librarian. She has a BA in Mathematics from the University of Kansas and an MLS from Rutgers University.

© 1989 by The Haworth Press, Inc. All rights reserved.

58   COLLECTION MANAGEMENT IN SCI-TECH LIBRARIES

spread. After explaining in greater detail the relationships between the three topics, a list of important monographic and serial titles will be provided as a guide to the selector.

The task of science is the description, cataloging, explanation and clarification of natural or artificial phenomena with a view to their prediction and control. The field of dynamical systems studies the aspect of phenomena in which nonlinearity is central. Chaos is another term generally used to refer to these rapid nonlinear changes. Without a mathematical definition, one can visualize nonlinearity in terms of explosiveness and sudden changes in matter, e.g., the mushroom cloud produced by a nuclear explosion, the eye of a hurricane, the disintegration of a cloud of smoke as it rises, the pattern of air movement around the wing of a plane in supersonic motion, or the random noise in a telephone line. Apart from observing that such phenomena present an explosive pattern, scientists could not say very much more before the 1960s. But the challenge was and is to reproduce some of these phenomena in a laboratory and, more importantly, to develop a language for detailed investigation, a theory with which the above diverse examples could be reduced to a few basic ones.

Mandelbrot was probably the first scientist who found a way of describing at least some of the above phenomena. Using a not-so-new mathematical idea of the ''dimension'' of a set of points in a plane, he could describe the difference between the jagged coastline of England and the jagged pattern of a lightning bolt. In other words, he could catalog some of these nonlinear phenomena using this idea. His book, *Fractal Geometry of Nature* (''fractal'' for fractured, jagged, broken), contains many computer-generated pictures resembling a particular phenomenon, such as a lightning bolt. Thus, Mandelbrot was the first to popularize the theme of dynamical systems in modern times. With his pictures and examples he irrefutably proved that here was something interesting and worthwhile for scientists to study.

Mitchell Feigenbaum, another dynamicist, in contrast had a different approach to the subject, a mathematical approach. His idea was to iterate a map or function and see what happens after, for example, 200 iterations. To his surprise and to that of other mathematicians, simple maps like the one from z to z*z + 1.4 yield astonishing pictures which are of the same class as those studied by Mandelbrot. An important lesson was learned, comparable to the idea of perspective. That is, simple maps can generate very complicated patterns. So, mathematicians found themselves with the task of finding out systematically what can be obtained by the iteration of simple maps, work that is going on at the present time.

The study of nonlinear phenomena by these new techniques is young. Consequently there is not yet an identifiable and well defined "core list" as exists in older fields such as topology or functional analysis. Thus what follows is at best a reasonable list of materials that can be considered core. The many recent volumes applying dynamical systems to such fields as physics, biology and chemistry have not been included, nor have the many conference proceedings. The guiding principle has been to assemble important titles on dynamical systems from the mathematician's point of view.

MONOGRAPHIC LITERATURE

Popular Treatments

Gleick, James. *Chaos: making a new science.* New York: Viking; 1987. 352p.

Peitgen, Heinz-Otto; Richter, P. H. *The beauty of fractals: images of complex dynamical systems.* Berlin: Springer-Verlag; 1986. 199p.

Rietman, Ed. *Exploring the geometry of nature: computer modelling of chaos, fractals, cellular automata and neural networks.* Blue Ridge Summit, PA: Tab Books; 1988. 191p.

Textbooks and Surveys

Abraham, Ralph; Shaw, Chris. *Dynamics, the geometry of behavior: Pt. 1, periodic behavior.* Santa Cruz, CA: Aerial Press; 1982. 240p.

Abraham, Ralph; Shaw, Chris. *Dynamics, the geometry of behav-*

60 COLLECTION MANAGEMENT IN SCI-TECH LIBRARIES

ior: Pt. 2, chaotic behavior. Santa Cruz, CA: Aerial Press; 1983. 139p.

Abraham, Ralph; Shaw, Chris. *Dynamics, the geometry of behavior: Pt. 3, global behavior.* Santa Cruz, CA: Aerial Press; 1985. 176p.

Abraham, Ralph; Shaw, Chris. *Dynamics, the geometry of behavior: Pt. 4, bifurcation behavior.* Santa Cruz, CA: Aerial Press; 1988. 220p.

Abraham, Ralph. *Foundations of mechanics: a mathematical exposition of classical mechanics with an introduction to the qualitative theory of dynamical systems and application to the three-body problem.* 2d ed. with revisions. Reading, MA: Benjamin/Cummings; 1981. 806p.

Arnold, V. I. *Catastrophe theory.* 2d rev. ed. New York: Springer-Verlag; 1986. 108p.

Arnold, V. I. *Dynamical systems* III. Berlin: Springer-Verlag; 1988. 291p.

Arnold, V. I. *Geometrical methods in the theory of ordinary differential equations.* New York: Springer-Verlag; 1988. 351p.

Arnold, V. I. *Mathematical methods of classical mechanics.* 2nd corr. printing. New York: Springer-Verlag; 1980, c. 1978. 462p.

Bai-Lin, Hao. *Chaos.* Singapore: World Scientific; 1984. 576p.

Devaney, Robert L. *An introduction to chaotic dynamical systems.* Redwood City, CA: Addison-Wesley; 1987. 320p.

Nemytskii, Victor V. *Qualitative theory of differential equations.* Princeton, NJ: Princeton University Press; 1960. 523p.

Schuster, Heinz G. *Deterministic chaos: an introduction.* 2nd rev. ed. Weinheim, Federal Republic of Germany: VCH-Verlag; 1988. 270p.

Shub, Michael. *Global stability of dynamical systems.* Englewood Cliffs, NJ: Prentice-Hall; 1986. 150p.

Thirring, Walter E. *A course in mathematical physics. v. 1, classical dynamical systems.* New York: Springer-Verlag; 1978. 258p.

Thompson, J. M. T. *Nonlinear dynamics and chaos: geometrical methods for engineers and scientists.* Repr. with corrections. New York: Wiley; 1987, c. 1986. 376p.

Monographs

Adler, Roy L. *Topological entropy and equivalence of dynamical systems*. Providence: American Mathematical Society; 1979. 84p.

Birkhoff, George D. *Dynamical systems*. rev. ed. Providence, RI: American Mathematical Society; 1966. 305p.

Casti, J. L. *Dynamical systems and their applications*. New York: Academic Press; 1977. 240p.

Casti, J. L. *Linear dynamical systems*. Boston: Academic Press; 1987. 351p.

Collet, Pierre. *Iterated maps on the interval as dynamical systems*. Boston: Birkhauser; 1980. 248p.

Cook, Peter A. *Nonlinear dynamical systems*. Englewood Cliffs, NJ; Prentice-Hall; 1986. 216p.

Falconer, K. J. *The geometry of fractal sets*. Cambridge: Cambridge University Press; 1985. 162p.

Feder, Jens. *Fractals*. New York: Plenum Press; 1988. 283p.

Freidlin, Mark I. *Random perturbations of dynamical systems*. New York: Springer-Verlag; 1984. 326p.

Guckenheimer, John. *Dynamical systems*. Boston: Birkhauser; 1980. 289p.

Guckenheimer, John. *Nonlinear oscillations, dynamical systems, and bifurcations of vector fields*. New York: Springer-Verlag; 1983. 453p.

Hirsch, Morris; Smale, Stephen. *Differential equations, dynamical systems, and linear algebra*. New York: Academic Press; 1974. 358p.

Irwin, Michael C. *Smooth dynamical systems*. London: Academic Press; 1980. 259p.

Kifer, Yuri. *Random perturbations of dynamical systems*. Boston: Birkhauser; 1988. 294p.

LaSalle, Joseph P. *The stability of dynamical systems*. Philadelphia: Society for Industrial and Applied Mathematics; 1976. 76p.

MacFarlane, Alastair G. J. *Dynamical system models*. London: Harrap; 1970. 503p.

Mandelbrot, Benoit B. *Les objets fractals: forme, hasard et dimension*. 2d ed. rev. Paris: Flammarion; 1984. 203p.

62   COLLECTION MANAGEMENT IN SCI-TECH LIBRARIES

Mandelbrot, Benoit B. *Fractals: form, chance & dimension*. San Francisco: W. H. Freeman; 1977. 365p.

Mandelbrot, Benoit B. *The fractal geometry of nature*. New York: W. H. Freeman; 1983. 468p.

Moser, Jurgen. *Stable and random motions in dynamical systems: with special emphasis on celestial mechanics*. Princeton, NJ: Princeton University Press; 1973. 198p.

Ornstein, Donald. *Ergodic theory, randomness, and dynamical systems*. New Haven: Yale University Press; 1974. 141p.

Palis Junior, Jacob. *Geometric theory of dynamical systems*. New York: Springer-Verlag; 1982. 198p.

Sagdeev, R. Z. *Nonlinear physics: from pendulum to turbulence and chaos*. 3 vols. New York: Gordon and Breach; 1988.

Seydel, Rudiger. *From equilibrium to chaos: practical bifurcation and stability analysis*. New York: Elsevier; 1988. 367p.

Siegel, Carl L.; Moser, Jurgen. *Lectures on celestial mechanics*. rev. ed. New York: Springer-Verlag; 1971. 290p.

Smale, Steve. *The mathematics of time*. New York: Springer-Verlag; 1980. 151p.

Tomiyama, Jun. *Invitation to C^*-algebras and topological dynamics*. Singapore: World Scientific; 1987. 167p.

Walker, John A. *Dynamical systems and evolution equations: theory and applications*. New York: Plenum Press; 1980. 236p.

Wiggins, Stephen. *Global bifurcations and chaos*. New York: Springer-Verlag; 1988. 494p.

West, Bruce J. *An essay on the importance of being nonlinear*. Berlin: Springer-Verlag; 1985. 205p.

Journals

Although journal literature is vitally important to the study of mathematics, the concerted study of nonlinearity is so new that the literature is widely scattered through many important mathematics journals. However, two journals have as their primary focus the publication of articles in this field:

Ergodic Theory and Dynamical Systems. Cambridge: Cambridge University Press; 1981 – .

Nonlinearity. Bristol, UK: Institute of Physics and the London Mathematical Society; 1988 – .

Humanities and Social Sciences Librarians in the Science-Engineering Library: Utilization and Implications for Effective Collection Development and Reference Services

Donald G. Frank
Christine Kollen

SUMMARY. With capable assistance and formal training, the humanities or social sciences librarian can provide effective bibliographic services in a science-engineering library. Essential skills employed in the intellectual process of collection development can be refined and applied. Quality of reference assistance is not necessarily reduced by the absence of academic credentials in the scientific or technical disciplines.

INTRODUCTION

Is it possible for a professional librarian, educated in the humanities or social sciences, to provide effective bibliographic services in a major science-engineering library? Or, is it necessary for a science-engineering librarian to have an academic degree in science or technology? Approximately 50% of the librarians in science-engi-

---

Donald G. Frank is Head, Science-Engineering Library, University of Arizona, Tucson, AZ 85721. He received the BS (Mathematics) at Southeast Missouri State University, the MALS at the University of Missouri, and the MPA at Texas Tech University. Christine Kollen is Reference Librarian, Map Collection, University of Arizona, Tucson, AZ 85721. She received the BS (Geology) at the University of Washington and the MLS at the University of Arizona.

© 1989 by The Haworth Press, Inc. All rights reserved. *63*

neering libraries do not have degrees in scientific or technical disciplines.[1] Is the quality of bibliographic services affected if the librarians do not possess ''appropriate'' formal academic credentials? In this paper, we will examine the concept of quality with a focus on collection development and reference services. We believe that a scientific or technical education, while desirable, is not an essential criterion to achieve success as a science-engineering librarian. Problems associated with the utilization of humanities and social sciences reference librarians in large science-engineering libraries are discussed. Approaches and techniques to enhance the overall quality of bibliographic services are proposed.

COLLECTION DEVELOPMENT

Development and management of the library's collections is a complex process. The process of collection development encompasses a variety of intellectual activities organized to obtain the bibliographic materials needed to support instructional programs and faculty or graduate research.[2] Collection development methodologies may vary from one library system to another. In major science-engineering libraries, the reference librarians, or selectors, usually participate in the process of collection development. The degree of participation depends on the organization of the library system and the priorities assigned to the development of collections.

Proficiency as a selector of scientific and technical materials may be attained by the humanities or social sciences reference librarian. Knowledge of the procedures associated with collection development, an appreciation of the scientific and technical literature, and a sense of commitment are required.

Initially, the selector must understand collection development from an organizational perspective. Which librarians participate actively in the process of collection development and, specifically, as selectors of bibliographic materials? In some academic library systems, the activities associated with collection development are centralized within a particular department in which bibliographers are responsible for the selection of materials. Collection development may be decentralized in other academic libraries. Frequently, some combination of centralized and decentralized practices evolves, depending on attitudes toward and the philosophy of collection development, the overall structure of the library system, and the perceived bibliographic needs of relevant user groups. As the reference librarians in a science-engineering library are usually active participants in the program of collection development, they need to be aware of the roles of all personnel directly involved and the procedures necessary to recommend the acquisition of needed monographs and serials.

In the major science-engineering library, one of the librarians should be responsible for the primary activities related to collection development. While all of the reference librarians may participate in collection development, a "coordinator" is able to provide needed focus and direction. Selection of a coordinator emphasizes the importance of collection development. Important projects, such as a critical review of serial titles, can be organized and implemented by the coordinator. Also, continuing activities associated with education and training for selectors can be conducted by a coordinator.

In addition to understanding the organization and methodology of collection development, an intrinsic appreciation of the literature of science and technology is critical. While collection development is an intellectual process, a desire to become familiar with relevant policies and procedures and then a willingness to apply these in the development of collections are important factors. If one is motivated to recognize the importance of collection development, he or she is more likely to devote quality time to the activity. In particular, one needs to appreciate the special importance and significance of serial publications and conference proceedings in the science-engineering library. Time, experience, and a resolute approach are required for the humanities or social sciences librarian to become a capable selector of scientific and technical materials.

Conscientious efforts to comprehend the details of local collection development policies and the particular levels of bibliographic support for the various academic disciplines represented in the collections are essential. The reference librarian needs to be aware of current academic emphases and changes. Active participation in an effective program of faculty liaison will enhance the quality of col-

66   COLLECTION MANAGEMENT IN SCI-TECH LIBRARIES

lection development. As the librarian communicates with faculty members, he or she acquires a sense of the faculty's needs.

Informed decision making is a requisite for effective collection development. As an intellectual activity, collection development is dependent on the quality of selection decisions. These decisions need to be based on relevant selection criteria that encourage librarians to consider priorities. Rutledge and Swindler identify several selection criteria that are especially applicable for selectors in the science-engineering library, including subject, intellectual content, potential use, relationship to existing collections, language, and bibliographic considerations.[3] The subject is a critical selection factor. What are the primary academic or institutional emphases? Selectors of scientific and technical materials need to consider and balance subject priorities in relation to instructional and research activities in academic departments. While difficult to assess for some bibliographic materials, the question of intellectual content should be considered. Essential authors and titles need to be represented in the collections. Substantial contributions to the literature must be selected. Potential use of monographic and serial publications needs to be deliberated. The selector should be aware of current academic trends and interests and consider these relative to probable need. In the science-engineering environment, the potential use of serial publications is usually considerable. Relationship to existing collections assumes some knowledge of these collections. Intellectual integrity, appropriate balance, and degree of comprehensiveness are important selection factors that should be considered in this context. As a relatively large number of scientific/technical articles and reports are published in other languages, selectors must consider language as a relevant criterion for selection. Finally, bibliographic considerations such as publisher or sponsor should be examined.

In the science-engineering library, the various serial publications are perceived as essential by faculty and students. The nature of this importance influences the process of collection development. A librarian with experience and expertise in the humanities and social sciences may not be intrinsically aware of this critical importance. In the discipline of history, for example, the monographic literature is perceived as desirable and necessary. While monographs are not

Donald G. Frank and Christine Kollen

unimportant in science and technology, the periodical literature is considered to be crucial for instruction and research. Currency of information is essential. The librarian must be aware of these differences in approach and use to be an effective selector of bibliographic materials.

In addition to an appreciation of the need for current serial publications, the selector must appreciate and understand the problems associated with serious serials inflation. Serials reviews are being conducted regularly in an increasing number of academic institutions. Implications for the science-engineering library are not good. Those who participate in a review of serial titles need to be familiar with the scientific and technical periodical literature and with the relevant criteria used to determine possible cancellations.

The increasing importance of collection development in academic libraries is reflected in the time devoted to this primary activity. Selectors of scientific and technical materials must acquire a practical knowledge of the collections and the unique user requirements in the major science-engineering library. With a positive attitude and sincere attention to collection development as an important intellectual process, the humanities or social sciences reference librarian will be able to attain an acceptable degree of proficiency as a selector.

THE REFERENCE FUNCTION

In reference services, quality is dependent on several variables. Generally, the degree of quality varies with the experience and expertise of reference personnel, the scope and depth of available collections, and the perceived importance of or commitment to the reference function. How important is expertise?

Will the humanities or social sciences reference librarian be able to identify with the bibliographic needs of faculty members whose research focus is in science and technology? Effective communication is critical in reference interactions. Krupp asserts that faculty members may lose a measure of confidence in the librarian's ability to provide capable reference assistance if the librarian is unable to comprehend basic terminology. Despite the possibility of losing face with library users, librarians with or without education/experi-

68 COLLECTION MANAGEMENT IN SCI-TECH LIBRARIES

ence in science and technology must not be afraid to state "I do not know" or "I am not sure" during the reference interaction.[4] Attempts at clarification are critical. If possible, the query might be referred to another reference librarian. Regardless of who "answers" or completes the reference transaction, sincere efforts to communicate with the patron will promote effective reference services. "Rapport is an essential reader relationship for successful reference work, especially in rather specific science subject areas. Unhappily it is frequently not developed."[5]

The reference librarian should be encouraged to refer "difficult" questions to other librarians whenever feasible. A functional referral system is a prerequisite for effective reference services and needs to be emphasized. If another reference librarian who may be more qualified to work with a particular question is available, then this librarian should participate in the total reference interaction. First-rate bibliographic assistance for the user is the primary goal. This referral process is especially critical for the humanities or social sciences librarian who is providing reference assistance in a scientific/technical environment. Such a process must be refined and supported by the librarian responsible for reference services. Reference librarians should feel free to refer appropriate questions.

Reference librarians need to be able to "place" reference questions within an appropriate "field" or discipline. It is a process that becomes refined with experience. As the inexperienced public services librarian learns to place questions within a particular context, he or she gains confidence. Many reference questions may be categorized by discipline with relative ease. Some questions, however, are not easily classified. In science and technology, a significant number of questions are not readily defined into specific subject categories. Other questions may fall into several categories. Determination of the appropriate discipline for these reference questions can be a difficult task for any reference librarian. The librarian with credentials in the humanities or social sciences may struggle with this process. During the initial phase of a good training program, this possibility needs to be considered. We should not assume that public services librarians are able to consistently place subject-oriented reference queries into particular categories. An effective identification with the scientific and technical disciplines in repetitive reference situations requires time and conscientious efforts.

FORMAL ORIENTATION AND TRAINING

A creditable program of orientation and training will facilitate the educational process for the librarian with academic credentials in the humanities or social sciences. Too frequently, the training received by public services librarians is basically "on-the-job" in nature. This approach may be inadequate. A formal and rigorous program of orientation and training, with enthusiastic administrative support, should be operational. Both attitude and performance are enhanced by formal training. The direct relationship between attitude and performance underlies the need to devote necessary and sufficient time to orientation and training.

Initially, in an orientation/training program, one needs to be aware of any actual or potential apprehensions over the perceived complexities associated with science or technology. Occasionally, students are conditioned to fear the fundamental concepts related to mathematics, chemistry, physics, and other sciences. The librarian who is responsible for orientation and training should realize that this propensity may exist. In these instances, a significant measure of patience and understanding is required during the training process.

As the reference librarian proceeds in a program of education and training, he or she should be aware of the philosophical principles on which scientists operate. It is important to attain a fundamental understanding of the scientific approach or methodology. How do scientists attempt to satisfy information needs? What are the critical elements in the research process? According to Medawar, research encompasses "all exploratory activities of which the purpose is to come to a better understanding of the natural world."[6] Additionally, "science is a logically connected network of theories that represents our current opinion about what the natural world is like."[7] Some understanding of general scientific methodology facilitates the

COLLECTION MANAGEMENT IN SCI-TECH LIBRARIES

training process and promotes an appreciation of the research efforts of faculty members.

It is possible, and not necessarily difficult, to become familiar with the terminology associated with a scientific or technical discipline. The librarian with minimal expertise in science and technology should be encouraged to attain this understanding. Guides to the specific nomenclature and to important literature are available for most disciplines. These are valuable reference tools that should be noted at the beginning of the training program. The activities and duties related to faculty liaison and collection development will promote general comprehension of the terminology. Additionally, as the librarian assists and instructs faculty and students in reference interactions, his or her knowledge of the ''language'' of science and technology is enhanced.

An active program of orientation and training evolves with the librarians who participate in the program. This needs to be recognized by program coordinators who are concerned with the professional development of reference personnel. As bibliographic programs and services and associated priorities change, these modifications need to be reflected in a progressive program of education and training. An up-to-date training manual is essential. The training manual is a primary source of relevant policy and procedures. If the librarian participating in the training program is responsible for updating and revising relevant policies and procedures, the importance of the training process will be reinforced.

CONCLUSION

With capable assistance and formal training, the humanities or social sciences librarian will provide effective bibliographic services in a scientific/technical academic environment. Essential skills employed in the intellectual process of collection development may be refined and applied. Quality of reference services is not necessarily reduced by the absence of academic credentials in the scientific or technical disciplines. A positive attitude is a requisite for success. Patience and a willingness to be flexible are crucial elements in a rigorous training program. In addition to administrative attention and support, all members of the reference staff must be willing to contribute to the professional growth and development of a colleague. If necessary, mentoring relationships can be established. Hopefully, the librarian will realize that mistakes are permitted and be encouraged to learn and to grow. If such an open environment is cultivated, the likelihood of professional success will be significantly enhanced, in spite of the lack of a degree in science or engineering.

NOTES

1. Mount, Ellis. *University science and engineering libraries*. 2d ed. Westport, CT: Greenwood Press; 1985: p. 50.

2. Cline, Hugh F.; Sinnott, Loraine T. *Building library collections: policies and practices in academic libraries*. Lexington, MA: Lexington Books; 1981: p. 2.

3. Rutledge, John; Swindler, Luke. The selection decision: defining criteria and establishing priorities. *College & Research Libraries*. 48(2): 123-131; 1987 March.

4. Krupp, Robert G. What education is best? *Science & Technology Libraries*. 4(3/4): 105-109; 1984 Spring/Summer.

5. Krupp, p. 106.

6. Medawar, P. B. *Advice to a young scientist*. New York: Harper & Row; 1979: p. 1.

7. Medawar, p. 84.

SCI-TECH COLLECTIONS

Tony Stankus, Editor

The 1960s and 1970s saw many curricular experiments that forced disparate disciplines together. Alas, many of these academic marriages were contrived from the start and dissolved when the funding pipeline or education fashions no longer held them together. But the marriage called surface and colloid science remains happy for its partners from physics, chemistry, biology, and engineering backgrounds. The field has interesting historical roots, noted in this paper and the reinforcement of sustained interest. Demands and support keep coming from both hi-tech and consumer sectors. Instant photography and diet mayonnaise that doesn't have the texture of a substance that is largely water, are two examples of triumphs at the day-to-day end. Ever more narrowly etched computer chips are examples of the other more sophisticated end. This widespread interest requires the kind of collection advice that Tina Chrzastowski brings. Her colleagues at Illinois have long proved leaders in what has historically been America's most productive graduate department of Chemistry.

Information Sources in Surface and Colloid Chemistry

Tina Chrzastowski

SUMMARY. The basic principles and concepts of surface and colloid chemistry are of concern to many science disciplines, including chemistry, physics, engineering, materials science, biology and medicine. These same principles are used in the composition and production of consumer items such as plastics, glues, aerosols, creams, cosmetics and dairy products. The chemical, petroleum, mining, electronics and computer industries also employ surface science principles. This broad, interdisciplinary subject is represented to some degree in every library's science collection. This paper presents a brief background on surface and colloid chemistry and cites general sources in sections covering textbooks, monographic series, conferences, journals, indexes, current awareness tools, online databases and organizations.

INTRODUCTION

What do photocopies, bubble gum, shaving cream, marbled paper and salad dressing have in common? These and countless other everyday items employ the science of surface and colloid chemistry in their composition or production.

Surface chemistry is an interdisciplinary science which studies the forces, processes and resulting phenomena arising at the surface between two phases (i.e., the interface), one of which must be either liquid or solid. Surface chemistry is sometimes called a "two-dimensional science," since only the surface area is studied and

---

Tina Chrzastowski is Chemistry Librarian and Assistant Professor of Library Administration at the University of Illinois, Urbana-Champaign, IL 61801. She received the BA degree at San Jose State University and the MLibr degree at the University of Washington.

© 1989 by The Haworth Press, Inc. All rights reserved.

COLLECTION MANAGEMENT IN SCI-TECH LIBRARIES

surface thickness is not a concern. Often divided between "wet" and "dry" research, dry surface chemistry focuses on the solid-vacuum or solid-gas interface, while wet surface chemistry studies the liquid interface, including disperse systems (particles dispersed in a medium).

Colloids are disperse systems of a particular size, usually with one dimension less than a micron. Named by Thomas Graham in 1861, the word colloid is from the Greek root "kolla," meaning glue. Examples of colloids are sols, gels, emulsions and foams.

Studies in surface and colloid chemistry examine the same systems from different perspectives. Surface chemistry studies the surface characteristics of a material; colloid chemistry studies the array of particles at the interface.[1] It is difficult to separate this intimate relationship, and therefore surface and colloid chemistry are often collective topics in resource tools, journals, textbooks and monographic series.

This paper provides a brief background and addresses resources in the two fields collectively and individually. General sources in the science of surface and colloid chemistry are identified, including basic applications in engineering and physics. For applications in other sciences and industries, the literature of that subject, including the trade and technology literature, should be consulted.

Early History of Surface Chemistry

The first reported surface chemistry experiment was performed in 1762 by Benjamin Franklin. While sailing to London, Franklin observed a calming effect to the ocean waves when oil was spread across the sea surface. He reproduced this observation in an experiment at Clapham Pond, near London, with the same results: when oil was spread over the surface of the water it had the effect of calming waves and ripples.[2]

In 1882, John Shields performed a large-scale surface chemistry experiment at a harbor near Peterhead, Scotland. Shields' success in subduing hurricane-force waves by applying oil to the water's surface was based on his patent for a device to pump oil into harbors from undersea pipes.[3] This patent, issued in 1880, is the first surface chemistry patent. However, due to mechanical difficulties with this pumping system, Shields' patent was never developed beyond the experimental stage.

At the turn of the century, simultaneous experiments in Germany, England and France led to the description and quantification of surface films. Agnes Pockles, a young German girl with no formal higher education, used kitchen equipment to make significant advances in the measurement of the surface tension of surface films. Her work was published through the recommendation of the British physicist Lord Raleigh, who was also conducting surface-tension experiments. Meanwhile, in France (1903-4), Henri Devaux was the first to spread polymers as films.[4]

Research and development continued at a quickening pace in the new century. Surface chemistry's most significant event of the twentieth century occurred in 1932, when Irving Langmuir was awarded the Nobel Prize for Chemistry for his work in surface chemistry. His experimental, theoretical and practical research brought surface and colloid chemistry both scientific respect and public awareness.

Applications and Recent Research

A partial listing of the science disciplines which apply colloid and surface chemistry concepts would include: chemical engineering, petroleum engineering, aerospace engineering, physics, materials science, biochemistry, environmental science, analytical and physical chemistry, medical research, and biotechnology.

Not only these sciences, but virtually every industry employs the concepts and principles of surface and colloid chemistry in the composition and production of their products. For example, consumers of cosmetics, electronics, pharmaceuticals and food and dairy products are using goods that rely on the research and application of surface chemistry. A list of surface and colloid chemistry products would be seemingly endless and include such products as: detergents, glues, paper, rubber, paints, lotions, creams, aerosols, porcelains, insecticides, plastics, waxes and pastes.

Recent research in surface and colloid chemistry focuses on solid surfaces in ultra-high vacuum, chemistry and electrochemistry at well-defined surfaces, heterogeneous catalysis and all aspects of

COLLECTION MANAGEMENT IN SCI-TECH LIBRARIES

liquid-liquid and liquid-vapor interfaces.[5] Thin films and supercon-
ductivity, supercomputing and the space program are examples of
today's "hot" topics employing surface science.

Future Developments

With computer applications, surface properties can now be measured, simulated and manipulated with speed and precision. Current
techniques, theories and even basic philosophies may become obsolete as the pace of development quickens. New techniques are being
developed and specialized series and journals are being published to
present this research. The variety and volume of resource tools focusing on surface and colloid chemistry will continue to grow as
research and applications advance.

RESOURCE TOOLS

Library of Congress Subject Headings

To locate cataloged materials utilizing LCSH, use the following
headings:

Surface Chemistry
Colloids
Chemistry, Physical and Theoretical
Surface Active Agents
Surface Energy
Surface Tension
Surfaces (Physics)
Surfaces (Technology)

For related entries, there are also over a dozen "see also" entries
under both "Surface Chemistry" and "Colloids," including "Ad-
sorption," "Catalysis," "Capillarity," "Foam" and "Gelation."

Call Number Classifications

Surface chemistry is classed generally in Library of Congress at QD 506 and in Dewey Decimal at 541.345. Colloid chemistry is classed in Library of Congress at QD 549 and in Dewey Decimal at 541.345, with Surface chemistry.

Serial and Monographic Tools

Books in Print lists currently available materials on this topic under: Surface Chemistry, Surface Active Agents, Surfaces (Physics) and Surfaces (Technology). *Ulrich's International Periodicals Directory* lists journals on surface and colloid chemistry under: Chemistry — Physical Chemistry, Chemistry — Organic Chemistry, and Physics.

Publisher's Catalogs

The American Chemical Society's *Annual Catalog* lists publications on surface chemistry in a section titled "Chemistry, Physical/Colloid and Surface." This subject listing includes subheadings for new and backlist titles, periodicals, multi-media courses and titles published by the Royal Society of Chemistry. Plenum's annual catalog in physical sciences and engineering uses the heading "Chemistry, Surface and Colloid Science." Other major publishers of surface chemistry titles such as VCH, Springer-Verlag and Elsevier, to name a few, publish catalogs using "Chemistry" as the general subject heading supplemented by author/title/keyword indexes.

TEXTBOOKS

These works describe in detail the basic principles of surface and colloid chemistry. Many were written to supplement general physical chemistry texts, which are too broad to include a detailed examination of surface science. Each book presents introductory material, general discussions, and graduate-level material on the subject of surface and/or colloid chemistry.

Monographs in specialized surface and colloid chemistry topics are interdisciplinary and multitudinous. These works can be located

80 COLLECTION MANAGEMENT IN SCI-TECH LIBRARIES

through *Books in Print*, through an online search, or through searching print indexes such as *Chemical Abstracts*. Monographs are included in the literature of each subdiscipline, and are too numerous and specific to include here.

Adam, Neil Kensington. *The physics and chemistry of surfaces*. 3d ed. London: Oxford University Press; 1941. No longer in print.

Adamson, Arthur W. *Physical chemistry of surfaces*. 4th ed. New York: Wiley & Sons; 1982.

Fridrikhsberg, D. A.; translated by G. Lieb. *Course in colloid chemistry*. Moscow: Mir; 1986.

Goodwin, J. W. *Colloidal dispersions*. London: Royal Society of Chemistry; 1982.

Heimenz, Paul C. *Principles of colloid and surface chemistry*. 2d ed. New York: Marcel Dekker, Inc.; 1986.

Hunter, R. J. *Foundations of colloid science. Vol.1.* Oxford: Clarendon Press; 1987.

Jaycock, M. J.; Parfitt, G. D. *Chemistry of interfaces*. New York: Wiley; 1983.

Miller, C. A.; Neogi, P. *Interfacial phenomena, equilibrium and dynamic effects*. New York: Marcel Dekker, Inc.; 1985. No longer in print.

Osipow, Lloyd I. *Surface chemistry: theory and industrial applications*. Huntington, NY: R. E. Krieger Publishing Co.; 1972. No longer in print.

Rideal, Eric K. *An introduction to surface chemistry*. 2d ed. Cambridge: The University Press; 1930. No longer in print.

Shaw, Duncan J. *Introduction to colloid and surface chemistry*. London: Butterworth; 1981.

Somorjai, Gabor A. *Chemistry in two dimensions: surfaces*. Ithaca: Cornell University Press; 1981.

Somorjai, Gabor A. *Principles of surface chemistry*. Englewood Cliffs, NJ: Prentice-Hall; 1972. No longer in print.

Woodruff, D. P.; Delchar, T. A. *Modern techniques of surface science*. Cambridge: Cambridge University Press; 1986.

Zangwill, Andrew. *Physics at surfaces*. Cambridge: Cambridge University Press; 1988.

MONOGRAPHIC SERIES

Series are important sources in surface and colloid chemistry, as many conference proceedings are published in this format. The most recent publication in each series is noted with the volume and date of publication. "R" designates a review series.

Advances in Surface Treatments. New York: Pergamon Press; v.4, 1987. An international series describing surface treatments and their effect on the behavior of engineering materials.

Advances in the Mechanics and Physics of Surfaces. New York: Harwood Academic Publishers; v.3, 1986. This series includes articles on friction, wear, adhesion and other processes occurring at the free surface of materials. For engineering and physics collections.

Colloid and Interface Science. New York: Academic Press; v.5, 1976. Irregular series based on papers presented at the International Conference on Colloids and Surfaces.

Colloid Science (R). London: Royal Society of Chemistry; v.4, 1983. Review articles on colloid literature published in the previous five years (Volume 4 covers 1977-81).

Progress in Colloid and Polymer Science. New York: Springer-Verlag; v.75, 1987. This series reports papers or conference reports on recent advances in colloid science.

Progress in Surface and Membrane Science. New York: Academic Press; v.14, 1981. This series is designed to bring together all aspects of general surface studies. Began as *Recent Progress in Surface Science*. No future volumes planned at this time.

Springer Series in Surface Sciences. New York: Springer-Verlag; v.8, 1987. Recent volumes have reported international conference proceedings on surface science topics.

Studies in Surface Science and Catalysis. New York: Elsevier; irregular, v.37, 1988. This series focuses on all aspects of surfaces and catalysis; up to three monographs per year are published, including annual reviews of catalytic and surface research.

Surfactant Science Series. New York: Marcel Dekker, Inc.; v.27, 1988. Each volume of this series is devoted to the applications, properties and analysis of surfactants.

82   COLLECTION MANAGEMENT IN SCI-TECH LIBRARIES

Surface and Colloid Science (R). New York: Plenum Press; v.14, 1987. Critical reviews describing the systems, theories and processes of surface science. Published annually.

A number of additional series address general physical chemistry topics and include important reviews, annual reports, or publish entire monographs on surface science research.

ACS Monograph Series. Washington, DC: The American Chemical Society; v.185, 1986. This series covers chemistry topics including surface and colloid chemistry. Indexed in *Chemical Abstracts*.

Advances in Chemical Physics. New York: John Wiley & Sons; v.72, 1988. Selected topics in physical chemistry, including surface science. Index is available for Vols. 1-55 (up to and including 1985).

Advances in Chemistry. Washington, DC: The American Chemical Society; v.217, 1987. Another ACS general chemistry series, again offering selected monographs in surface science. Indexed in *Chemical Abstracts*, and listed in the ACS Annual Catalog.

Annual Reports on the Progress of Chemistry C: Physical Chemistry. London: Royal Society of Chemistry; v.83, 1986. Reports the year's progress in physical chemistry. Current publication is two years behind.

Annual Review of Physical Chemistry (R). Palo Alto, California: Annual Reviews Inc.; v.38, 1987. Review articles on a wide range of physical chemistry topics, including surface science.

Springer Series in Chemical Physics. New York: Springer-Verlag; v.47, 1987. This series publishes the proceedings of a variety of conferences on surface science, as well as other topics in surface and colloid chemistry. Includes selected review articles.

CONFERENCES

In such a broad, interdisciplinary science, literally hundreds of conferences are held each year relating to surface and colloid chemistry. Individual conference topics might include thin films, reprographics, magnetic resonance, protein interfaces, lasers or electrochemistry. Subjects for conferences in surface science might overlap engineering, physics, chemistry, biology or medicine; industrial applications are addressed in still more conferences.

Conference proceedings can be located through indexes and abstracts, both in print and through online searching (see Indexes and Abstracts section). *Chemical Abstracts* routinely indexes conference literature, as do most services. Many symposia, proceedings and conference reviews are published in monographic series, journals or as monographs. These type of publications will also be included in the major indexes. Additionally, surface science topics will be included in the conference series listed here.

ACS Symposium Series. Washington, DC: The American Chemical Society; v.1 −; 1974 −.

AIP Conference Series. New York: American Physics Institute; v.1 −; 1970 −.

NATO ASI Series B: Physics. New York: Plenum; v.1 −; 1974 −.

NATO ASI Series C: Mathematical and Physical Sciences. Dordrecht: Kluwer Academic; v.1 −; 1973 −.

NATO ASI Series E: Applied Sciences. Dordrecht: Kluwer Academic; v.1 −; 1974 −.

JOURNALS

Journal literature is of utmost importance to chemists, who have the highest journal citation rate in the sciences, 93.6%.[6] Table 1 shows the most frequently cited journals in surface and colloid chemistry, identified by *Science Citation Index* and *Chemical Abstracts Service Source Index*. The journals listed below feature surface science articles in chemistry, physics and engineering.

Advances in Colloid and Interface Science. New York: Elsevier; v.1 −; 1967 −. This is an international journal covering interfacial and colloid chemistry topics with applications in biology, physics, chemistry and industry.

Table 1. Most frequently cited journals in surface and colloid chemistry.

Title	ISI Impact Factor	ISI Ranking Physical Chemistry	ISI Overall Ranking	Chemical Abstracts Overall Ranking
Progess in Surface Science	3.640	3	166	>1000
Surface Science	3.176	6	216	32
Journal of Physical Chemistry	2.967	7	252	10
Advances in Colloid and Interface Science	2.200	12	427	>1000
Langmuir	2.153	13	447	415
SIA:Surface and Interface Analysis	2.000	14	498	>1000
Journal of Colloid And Interface Science	1.385	25	866	143
Applied Surface Science	1.277	27	953	724

Colloids and Surfaces	.859	38	>1000	421
Progress in Colloid and Polymer Science	.785	40	>1000	>1000
Journal of Dispersion Science and Technology	.492	45	>1000	>1000
Colloid Journal (USSR) (translation)	.159	52	>1000	>1000

Column 1. Impact Factor is the "measure of the frequency with which the 'average article' in a journal has been cited in a particular year."

Columns 1, 2 and 3. ISI figures are from Science Citation Index Journal Citation Reports, 1986, Volume 19.

Column 4. Chemical Abstract figures are from the Chemical Abstracts Service Source Index, quarterly supplement, January-December, 1987.

86   *COLLECTION MANAGEMENT IN SCI-TECH LIBRARIES*

Applied Physics A: Solids and Surfaces. New York: Springer-Verlag; v.1 –; 1981 –. Experimental and theoretical investigations and applied research are published in this journal, including topics in surface science, surface engineering and solid-state physics.

Applied Surface Science. Amsterdam: North-Holland Publishing Company; v.24 –; June/July 1985 –. "A journal devoted to the properties of interfaces in relation to the synthesis and the behaviour of materials." Continues *Applications of Surface Science* (Vol. 1-22/23, 1977-1985).

Chemical Reviews. Washington, DC: The American Chemical Society; v.1 –; 1924 –. This classic journal often reports on surface science subjects. The June 1988 issue is titled "Surfaces and Interfaces." Available online as a full database through STN or BRS.

Colloid and Polymer Science. Darmstadt: Steinkopf; v.252 –; 1974 –. "Official Journal of the Kolloid-Gesellschaft." Articles cover solid-state physics, colloid and polymer chemistry, biophysics, biology and medicine. Includes conference announcements. Formerly titled *Kolloid Zeit-schrift* and *Kolloid Zeitschrift & Zeitschrift fuer Polymers*.

Colloid Journal of the USSR. New York: Consultants Bureau; v.14 –; 1952 –. Translated from the Russian *Kolloidnyi Zhurnal*, and began with volume 14. Six-month time lag in publication of Russian articles, tables and charts included.

Colloids and Surfaces. Amsterdam: Elsevier Science Publishers; v.1 –; 1980 –. "An international journal devoted to the applications and principles of colloid and interface science." Contains research papers, brief notes, book reviews and announcements.

Critical Reviews in Solid State and Materials Sciences (R). Boca Raton, FL: CRC Press; v.1 –; 1970 –. Review articles in solid-state sciences including surfaces.

Journal of Chemical Physics. New York: American Institute of Physics; v.1 –; 1933 –. Broad scope for all aspects of physical chemistry, but section heading titled, "Polymers, Surfaces and General Chemical Physics" contains specific surface science articles.

Journal of Colloid and Interface Science. New York: Academic Press; v.21—; 1966— (formerly *Journal of Colloid Science*). Experimental, original research articles on colloid and interface chemistry. Includes occasional notes and book reviews.

Journal of Dispersion Science and Technology. New York: Marcel Dekker; v.1—; 1979—. Topics include dispersions, emulsions and phase equilibria in all applications. Papers, reviews and industrial news are published which focus on technological development and industrial applications.

Journal of Physical Chemistry. Washington, DC: American Chemical Society; v.56—; 1952— (published 1947-51 as *Journal of Physical and Colloid Chemistry*). Biweekly publication which includes a section heading titled, "Surface Science, Clusters, Micelles, and Interfaces." Also available as a full-text database online through STN and BRS.

Journal of Physics and Chemistry of Solids. New York: Pergamon Press; v.24—; 1963— (formerly *Physics and Chemistry of Solids*). Important journal for "dry" surface chemistry, as it addresses the solid interface.

Journal of Vacuum Science and Technology, Series A: Vacuum, Surfaces, and Films. New York: American Institute of Physics for the American Vacuum Society; v.1—; 1983—. An international journal focusing on thin films and surfaces; original research and review articles, as well as proceedings of AVS conferences and symposia are included. Six issues per year.

Langmuir. Washington, DC: American Chemical Society; v.1—; 1985—. Presents articles, symposium papers, letters, notes, comments and book reviews on a broad spectrum of surface and colloid chemistry topics. Also available as a full-text database online through STN and BRS. (See Introduction.)

Physical Review B: Condensed Matter. New York: American Physical Society, Ser.3; v.18—; 1978—. One of four parts, this section focuses on condensed matter, which includes surface science topics. Contains Rapid Communications and Brief Reports sections, as well as Cumulative Author indexes.

88 COLLECTION MANAGEMENT IN SCI-TECH LIBRARIES

Physical Review Letters. New York: American Physical Society; v.1—; 1958—. Short, concise articles designed for rapid publication. The physics and chemistry of surface are included topics.

Physics, Chemistry and Mechanics of Surfaces. New York: Gordon and Breach; v.1—; 1982—. This journal is a cover-to-cover translation from the Russian of *Poverkhonost. Fizika, Khimiya, Mekhanika*. Subjects are fundamental, applied and theoretical research; symposia, seminars and conferences are included.

Progress in Surface Science (R). New York: Pergamon Press; v.1—; 1971—. Review articles on interdisciplinary subjects associated with surfaces. Broad, international scope.

Reviews of Modern Physics (R). New York: The American Physical Society; v.1—; 1930—. This quarterly publication provides rapid publication of "scholarly" reviews.

SIA: Surface and Interface Analysis. London: Heyden & Son; v.1—; 1979—. Bimonthly journal reporting the development of techniques analyzing surfaces, interfaces and thin films, including their quantification and standardization. Contains articles, short communications and forthcoming events sections.

Surface and Coatings Technology. Lausanne: Elsevier Sequoia; v.27—; 1986— (formerly *Surface Technology*). Reports the science, technology and applications of coatings and surfaces which alter the properties of materials. For engineering collections.

Surface Science. Amsterdam: North-Holland; v.1—; 1964—. "A journal devoted to the physics and chemistry of interfaces" (from title page). Contains *Surface Science Letters* as a preface to the journal. A highly cited, important surface chemistry journal.

Surface Engineering. London: Institute of Metals and The Wolfson Institute for Surface Engineering; v.1—; 1985—. Incorporates *Surfacing Journal International*. This journal focuses on specific engineering applications; includes abstracts of current literature on surface engineering. For engineering collections.

Surface Science Reports (R). Amsterdam: North-Holland; v.1—; 1981—. This journal publishes "invited review papers on the properties of surfaces and interfaces of metals, semiconductors and insulators" (from journal scope).

Thin Solid Films. Lausanne: Elsevier Sequoia; v.1—; 1967—. Conference proceedings, original and review articles, letters, book reviews and announcements are included in this journal devoted to thick and thin films. For engineering collections.

INDEXES AND ABSTRACTS

In surface and colloid chemistry, the research topic application will determine the best index or abstract to choose. This section lists selected indexes and describes their organization, access points and coverage.

Chemical Abstracts. Columbus, OH: American Chemical Society; v.1—; 1907—. *Chemical Abstracts* is *the* major abstract for all chemical sciences. Published biweekly, *CA* has numerous indexes, including author, subject, molecular formula, and substance. The abstract is classed in 80 subject sections, including number 66, "Surface Chemistry and Colloids." "See references" are included in each subject sections for additional, related entries. *CA* indexes over 12,000 serials, and includes U.S. and international patents, conference proceedings, books, technical reports and dissertations. The *Index Guide* is an essential starting point for entry to the subject index. Entries are noted with explanations, previous headings, see references and definitions. *CA* is also available online (see Online Databases).

Government Reports Announcements and Index. Springfield, VA: National Technical Information Service; v.1—; 1946—. *GRA&I* indexes technical and research reports from the NTIS (National Technical Information Service) database. Biweekly indexes have subject categories and subcategories, as well as keyword, author, corporate author and contract, grant and report number indexes. These indexes are repeated in the annual cumulations. Keywords for surface science are "surface chemistry" and "colloids." The subject category and subcategory to use are "Chemistry—Physical and Theoretical Chemistry." Available online through Dialog, BRS and STN.

Index Medicus. Bethesda: National Library of Medicine; v.1—; 1959—. The subject organization of *Index Medicus* is based on "MESH"—medical subject headings. Headings include: Surface properties, Surface tension, Surface-active agents and Col-

90 COLLECTION MANAGEMENT IN SCI-TECH LIBRARIES

loids. *Index Medicus* is published monthly with annual cumulative indexes, and covers journal literature only. Available online as "Medline."

Engineering Index. New York: Engineering Information; v.1 −; 1884 −. *EI* is, as the name implies, an abstracting service for selected engineering topics. Monthly abstracts, annual indexes and 3-year cumulative indexes offer abstracts in classified sections. Subject and author and author affiliation indexes are available. Headings in surface science include: "Surfaces" and "Surface Active Agents," both with subheadings and see references. Available online as "Compendex" and "Compendex Plus" (see Online Databases).

Physics Abstracts (Science Abstracts A). New York: American Institute of Physics; v.1 −; 1910 −. *Physics Abstracts* is a classified listing of physics-related abstracts. Classed generally under "Physical Chemistry," surface science topics are found under 82.65 (Surface Processes) and 82.70 (Disperse Systems). Coverage includes journals, conference proceedings, and selected dissertations and monographs. Subject indexes are produced twice a year. Available online by searching the INSPEC databases (see Online Databases).

Physics Briefs. New York: American Institute of Physics; v.1 −; 1979 −. Similar to *Physical Abstracts*, but more thorough coverage of dissertations, patents and monographs, as well as similar coverage in journal literature, reports and conference papers. Special emphasis is on "non-conventional literature and literature in Eastern languages" (from preface). Entries are classified by subject, with surface chemistry located under section 82.65 (Surface Processes), section 81.60 (Surface Treatments), and section 68.00 (Surfaces and Interfaces). Colloids and related materials are found under 82.70 (Disperse Systems). Issues are semi-monthly with semi-annual subject indexes. Author indexes are included in each issue. Available online through STN (see Online Databases).

Science Citation Index. Philadelphia: Institute for Scientific Information: v.1 −; 1955 −. This index offers both limitations and expanded horizons. The Citation Index allows users to trace research fronts through their similar bibliographies; the permuterm subject index is limited to words found in the titles of articles only. Wide science coverage, including important surface science journals. Cumulations are for 5-year periods; the forthcoming cumulation will be 1985-1989. Available online through Dialog (see Online Databases).

CURRENT AWARENESS TOOLS

Current awareness tools can help the surface scientist keep up with the literature without reading every journal cited above. In addition to these sources, a SDI search (a tailored bibliography automatically produced each month) on *Chemical Abstracts*, or any of the other databases listed in the next section, will keep researchers up-to-date on all types of current publications: journals, books, dissertations, patents, government publications, conferences or technical reports.

CA Selects. Columbus: Chemical Abstracts Service, dates vary, biweekly publication. This service offers abstracts from *Chemical Abstracts* tailored to specific topics, over 160 topics in all. Surface chemistry subjects include "Surface Analysis" and "Surface Chemistry (Physicochemical Aspects)." Colloid science topics are "Colloids (Applied Aspects), Colloids (Macromolecular Aspects), and Colloids (Physicochemical Aspects)." Subscribers receive biweekly listings of from 100 to 200 abstracts.

Chemical Titles. Columbus: Chemical Abstracts Service; v.1—; 1960—. *CT* is a biweekly table of contents listing and index of selected chemistry journals, including those of interest to surface and colloid chemistry. Author index and title keyword index are included.

Current Contents: Physical, Chemical and Earth Sciences. Philadelphia: Institute for Scientific Information; v.1—' 1961—. *Current Contents* publishes the table of contents for selected journals in various disciplines. Surface and colloid chemistry topics are listed in the section titled, "Physical Chemistry/Chemical Physics." Title word and author indexes and current book contents are included.

92   COLLECTION MANAGEMENT IN SCI-TECH LIBRARIES

ONLINE DATABASES

Surface and colloid chemistry are broad, interdisciplinary topics with applications in areas such as industry, medicine and pure research. The most comprehensive database to select for any chemistry topic is *Chemical Abstracts*. Other databases offer specific subject specialties which, although the results may overlap *CA* results, may prove useful.

CAS Online. Columbus: Chemical Abstracts Service; 1967 – . Equivalent to the print *Chemical Abstracts*, is available through STN, and through Dialog and BRS as *CA Search*.

Compendex. New York: Engineering Information, Inc.; 1970 – . Equivalent to *Engineering Index*, available through Dialog, BRS and STN. *Compendex Plus* (Dialog) includes published proceedings from the index *Engineering Meetings*.

INSPEC. London: Institution of Electrical Engineers; 1969 – . A portion of this database is equivalent to the print version of *Physics Abstracts*, and is available through Dialog, BRS and STN.

Medline. Bethesda: National Library of Medicine; 1966 – . Equivalent to *Index Medicus*, *International Nursing Index*, and the *Index to Dental Literature*. Available through Dialog, and BRS.

NTIS. Springfield: National Technical Information Service; 1964 – . Equivalent to *Government Reports Announcements and Index* (see Indexes and Abstracts) and available through Dialog, BRS and STN.

Physics Briefs. New York: American Institute of Physics; 1979 – . Equivalent to *Physics Briefs/ Physikalische Berichte*, and *Astronomy and Astrophysics Abstracts* (the latter only 1987 –). Available on STN.

Scisearch. Philadelphia: Institute for Scientific Information; 1974 – . Equivalent to the print *Science Citation Index*. Available through Dialog.

Table 2 compares results in five databases searching the phrase "(surface or colloid) (w) chemistry." *CAS Online* is the only database with a section heading for surface and colloid chemistry; this section heading ("66/SC") was substituted for the free-text search in *CAS Online*. For comparison, searches were limited from 1980 to the present.

These results show that unless the objective is a comprehensive bibliography, more specific keywords defining the topic should be chosen. For example, in Table 2, Column D, the phrase "heterogeneous (w) catalysis" was searched as a subset of the original search in Column A. These hits will be within the topic of surface or colloid chemistry, but will contain only those citations which also address the more specific subset phrase.

An additional advantage of online searching is to quickly identify conference proceedings or other specific document types. By crossing the search with a code for conferences (Table 2, Column C) the percentage of conference papers found in Column A is identified for each database. On CAS Online, document-type searches can also be restricted to patents, books, journal articles, technical reports and dissertations. Review articles can be found by combining the search with the word "review" using the Boolean operator "and."

ORGANIZATIONS

Research Laboratories

Surface science research laboratories are commonly funded by the U.S. or Canadian governments, the site host, and industry sponsors. These labs frequently support graduate-level research, sponsor conferences, provide continuing education for industry, and make the results of their research available through publications, reports and seminars. A list of U.S. and Canadian universities maintaining surface science research laboratories is provided below.

Clarkson University, Potsdam NY
    Institute of Colloid and Surface Science
Lehigh University, Bethlehem, PA
    Center for Surface and Coatings Research
Lehigh University, Bethlehem, PA
    Emulsion Polymers Institute
Montana State University, Bozeman
    Center for Research in Surface Science and Submicron Analysis
University of Maine at Orono
    Laboratory for Surface Science and Technology
University of Michigan, Ann Arbor
    Colloid Stability Laboratory

Table 2. Results of computer searches in six science databases selecting the phrase "(surface or colloid) (w)chemistry."

Database	A. Cites 1980+	B. Cites 1988	C. % of A=Conferences
CAS Online	44,799	3948	4%
Compendex Plus	1,680	29	22%
INSPEC	2,904	124	27%
Medline	33	0	0
NTIS	1,055	22	4%
Physics Briefs	329	47	3%

Database	D. A and Heterogeneous (w)catalyst	E. Date of most current record
CAS Online	15	7/88
Compendex Plus	1	6/88
INSPEC	11	2/88
Medline	1	1987
NTIS	18	3/88
Physics Briefs	6	7/88

Note: In CAS Online the section code for colloid and surface chemistry (66/SC) was searched. The searches were performed August 19, 1988.

COLLECTION MANAGEMENT IN SCI-TECH LIBRARIES

University of Michigan, Ann Arbor
   Surface Science Laboratory
University of Minnesota, Minneapolis
   NSF Regional Instrumentation Facility for Surface Analysis
University of Western Ontario, London, Ontario
   Surface Science Western
University of Wisconsin-Milwaukee
   Laboratory For Surface Studies

The U.S. government directly supports a research laboratory as part of the National Institute of Standards and Technology. This lab is the Center for Chemical Physics' Surface Science Division in Gaithersburg, Maryland. Research centers on surface measurement and surface physics.

Societies

A number of scientific societies sponsor research, hold conferences and publish materials in surface and colloid chemistry. The three major fields of interest, chemistry, physics and engineering, are represented by the American Chemical Society, the American Institute of Physics and the IEEE (Institute of Electrical and Electronics Engineers). Additionally, the ACS has a Division of Colloid and Surface Chemistry. Established in 1926, this division holds seminars, presents annual awards, and provides a forum for national topics in surface science.

NOTES

1. Heinmetz, Paul C. *Principles of colloid and surface chemistry*. 2d ed. New York: Marcel Dekker; 1986.

2. Giles, C. H. Franklin's teaspoonful of oil. *Chemistry and Industry*. 1616-1624; 1969 November.

3. Giles, C. H.; Forrester, S. D. Wave damping: the Scottish contribution. *Chemistry and Industry*. 80-87; 1970 January.

4. Giles, C. H.; Forrester, S. D. The origins of the surface film balance. *Chemistry and Industry*. 43-53; 1971 January.

5. Adamson, Arthur. A journal is born. *Langmuir*. 1:1-2; 1985 January.

6. Heinzkill, Richard. Characteristics of references in selected scholarly English literary journals. *Library Quarterly*. 50:352-365; 1980 July.

SPECIAL PAPER

Editorial Preparation
of the *International Dictionary*
of Medicine and Biology

Sidney I. Landau

SUMMARY. Describes the editorial work involved in preparing a three-volume dictionary for terms in medicine and biology. The ten years of effort are discussed, particularly the task of supervising a team of contributors and editors. Selection of terms and creation of definitions are emphasized.

The *International Dictionary of Medicine and Biology* (IDMB) was published by John Wiley & Sons in three volumes in January 1986 after more than ten years of preparation. The dictionary was well received. *Choice* called it ". . . essential for all hospital and medical libraries, and major educational institutions in the sciences . . ." (July/Aug. 1986), and *Nature*, the *New England Journal of Medicine*, and other scientific and professional library publications reviewed it favorably. IDMB is the largest medical dictionary in the

---

Sidney I. Landau is Editorial Director at Cambridge University Press (American branch) at 32 E. 57th St., New York, NY 10022. He received the BA degree from Queens College and the MFA degree from the University of Iowa.

© 1989 by The Haworth Press, Inc. All rights reserved. *97*

98 COLLECTION MANAGEMENT IN SCI-TECH LIBRARIES

English language, and one of the largest in any language, with more than 150,000 entries and nearly 160,000 definitions in 3,300 pages. The database consists of 27.5 million keystrokes and corresponds to 22 million printed characters. Seventy different subject areas are covered, ranging from anatomy to zoology and including comprehensive treatment of every medical specialty. Terms were selected and defined by 81 editors singly or jointly responsible for an entire subject, and assisted by a like number of contributing editors. An in-house staff at John Wiley & Sons under my supervision as editor-in-chief compiled this material and edited, cross-checked, and sometimes rewrote it. This paper will describe the chief steps involved in planning and producing the dictionary.

TRANSLATION EFFORTS

My involvement with IDMB began in September 1977, two years after the project was begun. In July 1975, Wiley had signed a contract with the French publisher Masson to acquire the English-language rights to Masson's four-volume *Dictionnaire Français de Médecine et de Biologie* (1970-75). The idea was simply to translate it. The original participants in this negotiation estimated that the work could be translated and published in two to three years under the editorship of a prominent medical doctor with one or two consultants. Thousands of individual French definitions, pasted on slips of paper, were prepared. The medical doctor, E. Lovell Becker, who had previously supervised the compilation of a nomenclature in nephrology, engaged a number of prominent subject specialists and simply sent the slips to them, asking them to translate the definitions into English. After two years, very little progress had been made, and Dr. Becker realized that the full-time attention of a professional lexicographer was needed.

I had been in lexicography since 1961, first as a definer, then as editor-in-chief of the Funk & Wagnalls dictionaries. In 1970 I joined Doubleday and edited *The Doubleday Dictionary* (1975) and the *Doubleday Roget's Thesaurus* (1977). Soon after I joined Wiley in 1977 I realized that the company's expectations of publishing a major scientific dictionary in a few years were utterly unrealistic. Moreover, it wasn't long before I also realized that the idea of translating a medical dictionary from the French was impractical and could not result in a dictionary that would be competitive in quality with the existing medical dictionaries in English.

Differences in medical nomenclature between French and English had already created numerous problems for the subject editors to whom Dr. Becker had sent French definitions. Many of the French lemmas (head words), when translated literally into English, corresponded to no known English medical term. Conversely, many thousands of common and uncommon English terms had no counterpart in the Masson dictionary. The French dictionary was far more encyclopedic than American dictionaries, with comparatively long descriptions of terms; but overall it included far fewer terms than the leading one-volume American medical dictionaries, which have about 100,000 entries. Some subject editors also complained that the entry list included a number of terms that had been obsolete in America for years, or that were based on outdated or discredited concepts.

Translating medical nomenclature is especially nettlesome because of the huge number of variant expressions for the same entity. For example, Henoch-Schönlein purpura is also known as allergic purpura, purpura abdominalis, acute vascular purpura, anaphylactoid purpura, purpura nervosa, purpura rhematica, Schönlein's purpura, Schönlein-Henoch purpura, hemorrhagic exudative erythema (obsolete), hemorrhagic capillary toxicosis, Henoch's purpura, Henoch's disease, Schönlein's disease, Schönlein-Henoch disease, Henoch-Schönlein syndrome, and Schönlein-Henoch syndrome. Usage varies from country to country. If a Frenchman had described this disorder at about the same time that Henoch and Schönlein (both Germans) described it, you can be sure the French would still call it by another name. Doubtless there are variants used in other languages that are not direct translations of any of the English variants listed above.

Let us assume a new strain of a disease is identified. If the original paper is in English and the disease is given an English name, the name of the disease will be translated into French, German, etc. But often, as translators know, a literal translation is not possible, perhaps because it corresponds in the second (or target) language to an idiomatic expression having an altogether inappropriate meaning.

100 COLLECTION MANAGEMENT IN SCI-TECH LIBRARIES

In such cases, the translator seeks to find an equivalent expression in the target language. Years later when someone wants to translate the French lemma into English, he may find no parallel in the English medical lexicon. Worse, seeking such a parallel, he may easily but mistakenly identify it with an altogether different disease which fortuitously but infelicitously resembles the literal English translation of the French lemma (a so-called false friend). Add to this confused state of affairs that even in English, there is no unanimity over preferred terms for many conditions (recall the dispute between the Americans and French over what to call the virus causing AIDS, finally resolved as HIV for human immunodeficiency virus), and you can see the practical impossibility of using literal translations to create a new dictionary.

ENGLISH LANGUAGE WORD LIST

I decided early on that we had to build our own word list independently of the French dictionary and simply use the latter as one of a number of potential sources. I also decided that it was fruitless to continue translating any French definitions and that we should have to compose all new definitions after having compiled the word list. We then set about compiling a word list that grew to over 220,000 terms by the end of 1978. We looked at very existing medical dictionary in English, at specialized glossaries and word lists (indexes of current textbooks were good sources), and other lists provided by the subject editors. To emphasize the importance of word list selection, each subject editor was paid a nominal fee for providing a word list. Compiling the word list was not simply a process of writing down terms, but of categorizing them by one or several subjects. A few months after I took over the project, I hired a managing editor, Ruth Koenigsberg, who was also an experienced lexicographer, and the two of us trained half a dozen free-lance medical editors in assigning subject codes to the word list. This work took about six months, and was completed in June 1979, by which time the list had been pared to 185,000 terms by the elimination of duplications and trivial variations of the same term. We also began a citation reading program of current medical publications to keep abreast of new terminology. We clipped every new term as soon as it appeared and pasted it on an index card with bibliographic data. These too were assigned subject codes and would be sent eventually to the appropriate subject editor for his determination as to whether they merited inclusion; if so, he was asked to provide a definition.

Concurrent with the compilation of the word list, I wrote a 60-page style manual setting forth in a single alphabetic format all the guidance I could provide to the subject editors, who though expert in their fields were not particularly adept at writing definitions. I could not, of course, expect the editors to read the manual, but it was there as a useful reference to remind them, for example, that a proper definition could not include any medical term that was not elsewhere defined in the dictionary. If they used such a word, they were asked to add the "word-not-in" to their word list as a lemma and define it, or, if it was really properly part of another subject area, to send us a note about it so that we could see that it was defined by the appropriate editor. In spite of this advice, "words-not-in" was one of our major problems. Time and time again editors wrote definitions containing words in their own specialties which were not included in their subject's word list. Our staff had to be constantly vigilant for "words-not-in," and we filled boxes of cards with such words awaiting assignment for definition.

The terms and subject codes of our word list were input in a computer which — after many months of planning and experimentation — automatically generated three-part defining forms with a variety of codes imprinted. (There is not space in this paper to describe the elaborate coding structure of each term and definition.) In October and November of 1979, we sent out 185,000 defining forms in large boxes to 72 editors (later increased to 81). One shipment of five or six boxes, destined for our tropical medicine editor then working in Papua New Guinea, was inadvertently sent to London (his regular residence), and I shall never forget my conversations and extensive correspondence with Emery Air Freight and the freight forwarders at Heathrow Airport regarding their forwarding to New Guinea. After many months of frustrating discussion and an exchange of letters worthy of a James Thurber story, I was assured that the boxes were forwarded, but they never arrived in Papua New Guinea, and ultimately we had to reprint several thousand forms and ship them again. I have often wondered at what state of soggy

102 COLLECTION MANAGEMENT IN SCI-TECH LIBRARIES

corruption those pristine defining forms have now arrived, perhaps by now constituting a new ecological curiosity, infiltrated by local flora and fauna that have made for themselves a happy home in our lexicon.

DEFINITIONS OF TERMS

Definitions were written during the six-year period 1980-85, but in spite of frequent communications and occasional personal visits with the editors, few definitions came in until 1981. After all, the editors were research scientists or clinicians and frequently had other writing obligations as well as administrative responsibilities, and certainly the very modest fees we were able to pay were no inducement to work. The motivation came from other sources: first, from the authority and influence of Dr. Becker and the outstanding editorial board of distinguished scientists — five in all — whom he had assembled to establish the overall policies of the work and to help him in enlisting the best subject editors available;* secondly, from the personal visits I paid to each editor. Establishing a personal relationship, I found, was essential. An editor asked to contribute a great deal of time for very little recompense must at all events be given special and courteous attention and not be treated as if he is simply an object of bureaucratic manipulation. He must also be persuaded that those asking him to make such a substantial sacrifice are motivated by more than the goal of adding to their company's profitability. Thirdly, written communications were frequent. I sent each editor and interested parties (including senior officers of my own company) semiannual newsletters. Fourthly, I personally reviewed in detail the first few defining attempts of each subject editor.

In spite of these measures, persuading the subject editors to begin defining was not easy, and persuading them to continue to wade through the hundreds and, in many cases, thousands, of terms to be defined was even more difficult. After their preliminary attempts were evaluated critically, they were on their own, and no further

---

*The other editoral board members were Sir John Butterfield, A. McGehee Harvey, Robert H. Hepinstall, and Lewis Thomas.

editing could be done of their definitions until their entire subject had been completed. The complex interrelationships of terms within a discipline made it necessary to have all the terms in a subject before editing it; otherwise, one would waste a great deal of time on assumptions that would later prove to be false. For·example, the editors frequently defined the same terms unwittingly under two or more lemmas. Often the preferred term would only become apparent to us because the editor used it in defining other terms. An editor might seem to prefer Henoch-Schönlein purpura over all other variants and define the term under this lemma, but the same editor might, in his own definitions of other terms, commonly use another variant, such as Schönlein-Henoch purpura. When we found that his usage conflicted with his judgment of preferred usage, we might query him on the point or, if other evidence also supported his usage (i.e., other editors also used that form of the term), we might conclude that his preference was not supported by common usage and change the preferred term accordingly. Such judgments are only possible when one has the complete body of definitions in a subject to work from; therefore, I made it a practice never to edit a subject until it was virtually complete. This practice, which might seem to have delayed the project's completion, actually accelerated it by avoiding costly mistakes that would later have had to be undone.

The problem of "words-not-in" used in definitions has already been alluded to. This was a very common error, and we generated thousands of new terms from spotting such words and asking the editors to define them.

Experts untrained in lexicography tend to delete terms simply because they happen to be unfamiliar with them. They imagine that because they are expert cardiologists (let us say) that there can be no cardiology term of any importance that they do not know. This bit of hubris must be tactfully expunged from their psyche. Above all, they must be made to understand that the *language* of cardiology is not cardiology, and that expertise in cardiology does not necessarily imply a perfect knowledge of the language of cardiology. Teaching humility to doctors is not easy, but this pretty well describes the task. Although they were indisputably the experts in their subjects, I made them understand from the outset that in matters of lexicography I was the boss. To most, this was a relief. It is essential in dealing with authorities to establish one's own editorial authority as absolute on one's own turf. This can be done in a way that is unthreatening and in fact supportive of the common goal of producing a book of the highest quality, both as to technical accuracy (their business) and as to professional lexicographical standards (my business).

Editors often uncritically defined any term assigned to them, even if it had been assigned to them by mistake and clearly belonged in another subject category. So, for example, a pediatrician might define a term in obstetrics or in nuclear medicine instead of returning it to us, as we asked, for reassignment to the proper editor. Such misassigned definitions were worthless and often conflicted with other definitions of the same term (under a slightly different lemma) defined by the appropriate subject editor. Sometimes, too, the same term quite properly applied to two or more different subjects. A term describing a form of cancer affecting the soft tissue of children might, for example, have half a dozen variants; two might have been assigned to oncology, two to pediatrics, one to rheumatology, and one to orthopedic surgery. All four editors, ignorant of the variants assigned others, would send in different definitions — each from his own perspective — of the same term. It was our job, first, to determine that these four definitions did in fact describe the same condition — often no easy task! This frequently required correspondence with the editors, who might differ among themselves. Secondly, if we determined that all of the definitions did in fact refer to the same condition, we had somehow to resolve the differences among the various definitions. Pending such determinations, all problems of this kind were relegated to a well-worn box labeled "CONFLICTING SUBJECT ASSIGNMENTS," or CSAs, as we called them. These were among the most vexing questions we had to resolve.

Although I constantly warned our editors against plagiarism, and even ordered a rubber stamp (COPYRIGHTED — NOT TO BE USED VERBATIM) which I liberally applied to all copyrighted glossaries sent to them, we had nevertheless to be constantly on our guard against definitions too closely fashioned from other sources. Very few cases of outright plagiarism occurred — one such caused me six months of extra work — but there were cases of editors who naively believed they could appropriate quite a bit of another's work with impunity. We did our utmost to discover and correct such close correspondences; on the other hand, we realized that many definitions could not be defined very differently from established sources without straining the sense or introducing an artificial or prolix quality. In some cases, a close correspondence had to be allowed because it was the natural way to define the term, and might reasonably have been arrived at independently even if the previously published work had never existed.

EDITING PROCESS

After all of a subject's definitions were in house, they were given to a staff editor assigned the task of editing it within a deadline based on the number of definitions and my estimate of the complexity of the subject. The editing of a small simple subject might take 2-4 weeks, that of a long and difficult one as much as 4 months. In the course of editing a subject, the staff editor decided which terms should be reviewed by a second subject editor. For example, the pediatric oncology term might be first defined by our oncology editor, but might then be sent serially to our pediatrics editor and our rheumatology editor as a check of its accuracy and completeness. About 70% of the terms were reviewed by at least one other editor, and many were reviewed by more than one. As editor-in-chief, I examined all of the reviewed definitions and decided what changes to make, if any, in the original definition.

Following the review stage, the original subject editor was sent a list of all of his assigned terms with the definitions as finally edited. Concurrently, our computer house printed out for us a complete set of second defining forms with all definitions imprinted. These were proofread and errors were corrected, often necessitating a third or fourth defining form. A copy of this second defining form was sent to our etymologist if the word was deemed suitable for etymology. A number of complicated computer data checks were made at this time. One was to make sure that all terms originally assigned to editors were either deleted or defined; we had to be certain that no terms were simply lost (like those in New Guinea). Another

106   COLLECTION MANAGEMENT IN SCI-TECH LIBRARIES

checked the reciprocity of cross-references: if term A said it was also called B, term B should tell the reader to look at term A for the definition. If it did not, we wanted to know why not. (Some such instances were legitimate, so the correction could not be automatic.) A number of other useful data checks were done, but all involved considerable editorial effort. The computer quickly brought to our attention many hundreds of errors or anomalies that it would have taken us months of painstaking (and hideously boring) work to uncover; nonetheless, each such putative anomaly had to be individually checked to see whether it really was an anomaly or merely a quirk of our computer program, which like most such programs captured some perfectly legitimate cases that were simply not typical.

Following the data checks, we implemented the corrections made by the subject editors on their edited and reviewed definitions. The final tape was then merged with the independently produced etymology tape, and the combined tape was sent to a compositor for translation to type codes that would produce page proofs.

At this stage we were able to begin final editing with online video monitors, thus greatly facilitating our control of the editing process. The page proof stages followed the normal book production pattern, but since the work had been thoroughly proofread at the second defining form stage, our task was to proofread only subsequent changes and to implement the changes brought to light by our various data checks.

The data checks, final editor check, and online editing stages occurred in 1985, and IDMB was published in January 1986. It was with enormous relief that we finally resolved all the remaining conflicting subject assignments, and I shall never forget with what solemn pleasure we discarded the last tattered carton bearing the much feared and hated appellation, CSA.

NEW REFERENCE WORKS
IN SCIENCE AND TECHNOLOGY

Arleen N. Somerville, Editor

Reviewers for this issue are: Kathleen Kehoe (KMK), Columbia University, New York, NY; Donna Lee (DL), University of Vermont, Burlington, VT; Ellis Mount (EM), Columbia University.

HEALTH SCIENCES

Dictionary of food and nutrition. By J. Adrian and others. Translated by B. Weitz. Edited by E. Rolfe and others. Chichester, England: Ellis Horwood; 1988. 233p. $52.00. ISBN 0-89573-404-4.

Locating information in the field of food science can involve searching through medical, biological, and agricultural sources. This dictionary brings together 3,000 terms from several fields, including many expressions specific to food science and human nutrition. Entries are brief, but a number of them are enhanced by charts and diagrams. The appendixes give compositions of familiar foods, but other publications offer more complete information on food content, for example Bowes and Church's *Food Values of Portions Commonly Used* (1985). Primarily for specialists and students working in food science and nutrition. (DL)

© 1989 by The Haworth Press, Inc. All rights reserved. *107*

108 COLLECTION MANAGEMENT IN SCI-TECH LIBRARIES

Dictionary of medical eponyms. By B. G. Firkin and J. A. Whitworth. Park Ridge, NJ: Parthenon Publishing; 1987. 591p. $48.00. ISBN 0-940813-15-7.

Entries include both definitions and short biographies of the people immortalized by the eponyms. The dictionary is limited to concepts encountered in internal medicine. Though the authors practice in Australia, they demonstrate a thorough awareness of American usage. Doctors, nurses, medical historians, and, particularly, librarians, will find this book useful. (DL)

Directory of biomedical and health care grants-1988. Phoenix, AZ: Oryx Press; 1988. 402p. $74.50. ISSN 0883-5330.

Provides a useful directory to more than 2300 funding programs which are health-related. The main entry for each program identifies the usual location information (including phone number) plus descriptions of grants, restrictions on applicants (if any), amount of grants, schedules for application and sponsor information. In order to facilitate locating particular grants there is a detailed subject index as well as a separate index by sponsoring organizations, arranged alphabetically. In addition there is a sponsoring organizations index arranged by type of organization (professional versus governmental). Topics range from Abortion to Women's Health Programs. Although mainly devoted to U.S. programs, there were several in Canada and a few in other countries. (EM)

Directory of preventive medicine residency programs in the United States and Canada. 5th ed. Washington, DC: American College of Preventive Medicine; 1988. 100p. $15.00. ISBN not given.

Though the *Directory of Medical Residency Training Programs* is the primary source for information on residencies, it lists only the major specialties. In order to identify residencies in sub-specialties, one must consult other sources, such as this one. The *Directory of Preventive Medicine Residency Programs* describes residencies in general preventive medicine, occupational medicine, public health, and aerospace medicine. Obviously, this book will help medical students interested in specializing in preventive medicine, but it is also of use to policy makers and researchers studying the status of training programs for preventive medicine. (DL)

New Reference Works in Science and Technology 109

Federal health information resources. Edited by Melvin S. Day. Arlington, VA: Information Resources Press; 1987. 246p. $29.95. ISBN 0-87815-055-2.

This directory describes federally sponsored health sciences agencies, projects, and programs, arranged and indexed by subject. Rather than simply explaining what each group does to justify its existence, this publication is unusual in that entries indicate what services each organization will provide for the general public. If a group runs a library or museum, the directory indicates hours open to the public. Even photocopying facilities are reported. Each entry also describes publications and computer databases supported by the various groups. An appendix contains information about computer databases and refers the reader to the entries describing the organizations which maintain each database. A new edition is planned for 1989. (DL)

Medical information sources: a referral directory. 5th ed. Edited by Arthur W. Hafner. Chicago: AMA; 1988. 78p. $19.95. ISBN 0-89970-320-8.

This publication was originally assembled by the AMA's Division of Library and Information Management to help them refer patrons to the appropriate sources of information. Organizations' addresses and phone numbers alternate with citations for printed materials (mostly AMA publications). Replete with cross references, this directory would be a good addition to collections of other health care directories. (DL)

The Oxford companion to the mind. Edited by Richard L. Gregory. New York: Oxford University Press; 1987. 856p. $49.95. ISBN 0-19-866124-X.

The articles in this fascinating volume range from one paragraph defining "future shock" to a 20-page tutorial on the nervous system. Most articles contain bibliographies. Many biographical entries appear and still more names are referenced in the generous index. Since this one volume attempts to cover much of psychology, neurology, psychiatry, and philosophy, entries are by necessity brief, perhaps too brief to benefit professionals in these fields. Of more interest to students and laypersons. (DL)

A research guide to the health sciences: medical, nutritional, and environmental. By Kathleen J. Haselbauer. New York: Greenwood Press, 1987. 655p. $44.95. ISBN 0-313-25530-9.

This annotated list of references describes over 2,000 sources and covers all aspects of the health sciences, including dentistry, veterinary medicine, and alternative health care. Sources for the layperson are mentioned where appropriate. Textbooks, handbooks, monographs, indexes and abstracts, dictio-

110 COLLECTION MANAGEMENT IN SCI-TECH LIBRARIES

naries, encyclopedias, computer databases, and AV materials are reviewed. A guide to research in all areas of health care can't help but be overwhelming. Unfortunately, the poor quality typeface used makes the guide even more imposing. Still, a worthwhile purchase for libraries likely to have access to the tools listed. (DL)

Scholarships and loans for nursing education, 1987-1988. New York: National League for Nursing; 1987. 73p. $8.95. ISBN 0-88737-380-1.

Between the drop in enrollment for undergraduate nursing programs and the growing demand for nurses, efforts to attract more students for nursing programs has increased. But it is still the nursing student who is faced with financing her or his education. Covering all levels of nursing education, from LPN to graduate study and postdoctoral research, this booklet describes both sources of aid specifically for nursing students, and scholarship and loan programs available for all students. A purchase for high school and public libraries with patrons interested in LPN and RN programs, but also for academic and hospital libraries serving nurses pursuing further study. (DL)

LIFE SCIENCES

Dictionary of behavioral assessment techniques. Edited by Michael Hersen and Alan S. Bellack. New York: Pergamon Press; 1988. *Pergamon General Psychology Series.* $85.00.

This is a quick reference guide to behavioral assessment techniques for researchers and clinicians. Written instruments, behavioral observation techniques, and physiological measures used in behavioral assessment are included. An effort was made to include scales appropriate for all age groups. The individual entries were written by researchers who are skilled in the techniques they describe. The entries are encyclopedia length and include the purpose, development, psychometric characteristics and clinical use of the particular assessment technique. An author index and a subject guide provide access to the entries. The subject guide lists the scales alphabetically, gives the state or trait measured and provides the technique's assessment modality. Given the broad interdisciplinary use of behavioral assessments, this volume would be of use to researchers in psychology, sociology, and child development. (KMK)

Escherichia coli and Salmonella typhimurium: cellular and molecular biology. Edited by Frederick C. Neidhardt et al. Washington, DC: American Society for Microbiology; 1987. 2 vols. $85.00 (set) or $75.00 (set). ISBN 091-48268-91 and 091-48268-59 (soft).

This is a comprehensive treatment of the molecular and cellular biology of Escherichia coli and Salmonella typhimurium. It is a textbook, a reference work, and a bibliographic resource. Each chapter includes an extensive bibliog-

New Reference Works in Science and Technology 111

raphy which includes all the major papers on the topic. This work was commissioned by the American Society for Microbiology. Frederick Neidhardt organized a committee which planned the volume, solicited authors, and edited the final volumes. This work is a significant service to the biological sciences community. It is far more than a handbook — it is a review and synthesis of all the research to date, in addition to being a valuable source of data. This set is a "must" for life sciences and medical research collections. (KMK)

Handbook of multivariate experimental psychology. Edited by John R. Nesselroade and Raymond B. Catell. 2nd ed. New York: Plenum Press; 1988. 966p. (Perspectives on Individual Differences.) $95.00. ISBN 0-306-42562.

This is a revised edition of the classic 1966 work. The first four chapters, which cover basic issues in experimental psychology and data analysis, have not been changed fundamentally. The remainder of the volume has been extensively revised to include the advances in multivariate techniques that have been developed over the past twenty years. This is a research level handbook written for readers with an extensive background in statistics. Consequently it is appropriate for advanced graduate students and research professionals. Although it was intended for use by social and personality psychologists, it would be useful to other social scientists interested in multivariate analysis techniques. (KMK)

Human polymorphic genes: worldwide distribution. Arun K. Roychoudhury and Masatoshi Nei. New York: Oxford University Press; 1988. 393p. $56.00. ISBN 0-19-505123-8.

This volume is a compilation of gene frequency data at polymorphic DNA regions in human populations. It includes frequency data at 362 loci in 180 human populations gathered from the original papers. The frequencies are grouped into seven classes — enzymes, proteins, blood groups, HLA Systems, immunoglobulin systems, DNA polymorphisms, and miscellaneous. Within each group the genes are listed alphabetically, and then the populations studied are listed alphabetically with the accompanying data. The book also includes appendices with worldwide frequency distribution maps, and an extensive bibliography. This data is used by human geneticists, evolutionary biologists, physical anthropologists and genetic counselors and would be useful in biological sciences and medical collections in academic institutions. (KMK)

Life sciences organizations and agencies directory. Edited by Brigitte T. Darnay and Margaret Labash Young. Detroit, MI: Gale Research Co.; 1988. 864p. $155.00. ISBN 0-810-31826-1.

This new Gale directory includes a broad group of life sciences organizations including: scientific associations, international organizations, research centers, consulting firms, government agencies, libraries, and educational institutions. "Life sciences" is defined here to include biology (except neurobiology), bio-

112 COLLECTION MANAGEMENT IN SCI-TECH LIBRARIES

technology, agriculture, ecology and the environmental sciences. There are approximately 7,600 listings; most of them were culled from other Gale directories such as the *Encyclopedia of Associations*. The directory contains 18 chapters organized by institutional type. There is a single index containing the associations' names and keywords. The index supplies reference numbers to the entries in lieu of page numbers. Although the book's price is high, it is an excellent reference source for special or academic life sciences libraries. (KMK)

SCIENCE, GENERAL

How to write and publish a scientific paper. 3d ed. By Robert A. Day. Phoenix, AZ: Oryx Press; 1988. 211p. cloth $21.95; paper $14.95. ISBN 0-89774-456-X (paper); ISBN 0-89774-472-1 (cloth).

A handbook for authors (and would-be authors) of sci-tech materials, including periodical articles, books, review papers, conference reports, book reviews and oral presentations. The author's style is friendly, down to earth and authoritative, so most scientists and engineers, no matter how experienced they may be in writing, would profit from reading the book. The author also provides lists of common errors in style and spelling, as well as lists of abbreviations and definitions. Includes information on such diverse topics as designing effective graphs and obtaining rights to include copyrighted materials from other publications. Should be suitable for all reference collections. (EM)

SCI-TECH IN REVIEW

Karla Pearce, Editor
Giuliana Lavendel, Associate Editor

CLEVER DATABASES

Anon. Tangling the web. *The Economist*. 308(7561): 82; 1988 July 30.

A type of software called hypertext organizes information more flexibly than a conventional database, and allows the computer to think in a lateral mode. The heart of hypertext is an automated cross-referencing system, allowing one to link anything with anything else, to help a reader work through a complex technical manual, or guide a researcher to see links between disparate bits of data. Carnegie-Mellon put hypertext technology to work to navigate the documentation of a nuclear aircraft carrier; Xerox's NoteCards helped writers research and write documents, Apple's Hypercard married simple hypertext to graphics. There are other programs like Owl for IBM computers, and Lotus's Agenda, which is defined as a "personal information manager." The public may be slow or unwilling to accept this unfamiliar technology, but the next generation of hyperstuff, hypermedia, is already in the wings, linking video and music as well as text and computer graphics. (GAL)

© 1989 by The Haworth Press, Inc. All rights reserved.

114 *COLLECTION MANAGEMENT IN SCI-TECH LIBRARIES*

JOURNAL OF COST-EFFECTIVENESS

Barschall, Henry H. The cost-effectiveness of physics journals. *Physics Today*. 41(7): 56-59; 1988 July.

Faced with the rapid increase in the price of scientific journals, decision makers are searching for some quantitative evaluation method to help weed subscriptions lists. Popular measures are the cost per printed character, which is approximately the same for physics, mathematics, and philosophy journals, and frequency of citation or "impact." The author tries to classify journals by both cost per character and citation frequency, concluding that the ratio of these two factors varies by three orders of magnitude. Causes for subscription price increases are listed, and possible solutions to the vicious circle of price increases followed by cancellations followed by more price increases. Reliance on page charges, accepting fewer papers for publication, electronic journals, and manuscripts in machine-readable form are among the suggested solutions. The American Institute of Physics believes that optical character recognition is more effective than compuscripts; it operates two Kurzweil systems day and night. (GAL)

LIBRARIAN EMPLOYMENT

Bering-Jensen, Helle. Plenty of jobs, too few librarians. *Insight on the news*. 4(24): 58-59; 1988 June 13.

The sixties saw a rapid growth of library jobs, which was followed by scarcity and oversupply of professional librarians in the seventies and eighties, when most of the new positions were replacements. As a consequence, enrollment in library schools fell dramatically, from 6,370 in 1974 to 3,538 in 1986: 1983 saw the lowest student enrollment. Now there are more jobs than graduates, and the need for librarians is greater, thanks not only to the explosion of information technology but also because of other factors. Public library systems have taken on more diverse functions; computer networks connect libraries in different sectors, creating new activities; corporations have set up their own libraries, staffed by "information specialists," and there are changes in the employment patterns of women. Eighty to 85% of public librarians, and 60 to 65% of their academic colleagues are women. Library jobs, like nursing and teaching, are suffering from the competition with better paying careers now open to women; wages are still modest, compared to those of other professionals. (GAL)

IMPROVED BOOLEAN RETRIEVAL

Fox, Edward A.; Koll, Matthew B. Practical enhanced Boolean retrieval: experiences with the SMART and SIRE systems. *Information Processing & Management*. 24(3): 257-267; 1988.

Boolean techniques have become the norm for information retrieval. But although popular, Boolean language typically retrieves just a fraction of documents relevant to a literature search. This may be due to the inherent ambiguity of the language, researchers' problems in identifying the topics of documents and searchers' misapplication of Boolean logic. The authors suggest additional techniques to improve search logic and more effectively index documents. These techniques include clustering related documents, feedback for relevance during the course of a search, ranking retrieved documents and assignment of weights to search terms. Experimental studies with the SMART and SIRE retrieval systems have shown their effectiveness in applying some of these techniques in order to enhance Boolean searching. (KJP)

LIKE TO BUY AN AIRPORT, A DAM?
THEY'RE FOR SALE.

Levin, Marc A. Government for sale: the privatization of federal information services. *Special Libraries*. 79(3): 207-213; 1988 Summer.

The current administration's strategy for shifting public functions to private enterprise or "privatization" is defined and discussed. One application of this policy, federal "contracting out," was tried at the National Oceanic and Atmospheric Administration central library in Rockville, MD, with disastrous results. According to the

COLLECTION MANAGEMENT IN SCI-TECH LIBRARIES

Chair of the House Civil Service Subcommittee on Human Resources, "this effort has cost the U.S. taxpayer far more money . . . than its privatization could possibly save." Costs and values for privatizing NTIS are also discussed. Information professionals are urged to remain skeptical about this program and mobilize to protect the "public information infrastructure." (KJP)

SERIALS PRICES

Mitgang, Herbert. American libraries are in crisis over the cost of scholarly journals. *The New York Times*. 137 (47,619): 11; 1988 Monday, September 5.

Administrators from the Research Library of the New York Public Library are quoted in their despair over rising journals prices. In 1987, the Research Libraries of NYPL spent over $3 million for periodicals and serials; this was spent for 30,000 periodical subscriptions and 120,000 serials. NYPL will be reducing their periodicals titles by 10%; and big ticket items such as *Biochimica et Biophysica Acta* and *Human Genetics* have been suggested as likely candidates. Budget woes from other large research libraries — Stanford, Harvard, Berkeley and the University of Michigan — are also noted. When they give reasons for the problems, librarians cite the weakened dollar and monopolistic publishing practices; publishers will cite the weakened dollar, the increase in information published and additional distribution costs. To address this problem NYPL is seeking greater private and public funding, as well as strengthening its collaborative arrangements with other research libraries around the country. (KJP)

FREEDOM OF INFORMATION SERVICE

Pell, Eve. And leave the FOIA to us. *Venture*. 10(8): 51; 1988 August.

Several years ago a Washington law firm specializing in food and drug regulations started processing FOIA (Freedom of Information Act) requests for customers who wanted help dealing with the agency, with some assurance of confidentiality. The firm started to set up a document delivery service (FOI Services, Inc.) near the FDA Headquarters, with the approval of the agency, which was burdened by requests from the public to provide copies of the same document over and over again. After a while, service emphasis changed from mere photocopying to organizing a knowledge base from the FDA and other federal agencies; FOI now has 70,000 FDA documents on file, all indexed in a database where terms like ibo-profen can be easily located. Recent policies have left the organization and delivery of information to the private sector, but it is now harder for FOI to identify and obtain documents from the federal government. (GAL)

INFORMATION CONTROL

Shattuck, John; Spense, Muriel Morisey. The dangers of information control. *Technology Review*. 91(3): 63-73; 1988 April.

During the past decade the federal government has placed restrictions on the availability of scientific and technical information, and attempted to shape its content. Through a series of policy directives, the executive branch has, according to the Harvard-based authors, effectively "restrain(ed) academic freedom, hamper(ed) technological progress and undermine(d) democratic decision making." They recognize that information is an important national resource, but note that governmental restraints on its communication have hurt American as well as foreign research efforts. Interpretations of laws from the Export Administration Act of 1979 to 1987 amendments of the Freedom of Information Act are described and their effects on research listed. Except where there is a clearly defined threat to national security, they ask for an executive order to "establish the presumption that information generated both inside and outside the government will be freely available." (KJP)

INFORMATION BROKERS

Webber, Julie. Information specialists can save companies time and money. *Infoworld* 2(22): 15; 1988 July 25.

Companies are learning to use outside information specialists rather than obtaining expensive subscriptions and having their own staff try their hand at online searching. Information brokerage firms have access to vast resources, online and otherwise. The average price range for a job is $300 to $500: this would include the search itself and relevant articles retrieved, plus phone consultations. Even companies like AT&T use information brokers for special tasks, like identifying conferences and consumer groups where a company speaker might be desired. Other companies use the information service when they are short on either time or staff. Client confidentiality is a big issue in the information industry. (GAL)

SCI-TECH ONLINE

Ellen Nagle, Editor

DIALOG SOLD TO KNIGHT-RIDDER

In an agreement signed on July 11, 1988, Knight-Ridder Business Information Services Inc. purchased Dialog Information Services from the Lockheed Corporation for $353 million. Industry speculation regarding the sale of Dialog had been widespread for several months, with several prominent information industry corporations reported to be among the ten major bidders. An asking price of $200 million had been initially reported. Dialog's revenues for 1987 were $98.1 million. Responses to the sale by key Dialog personnel were favorable. According to Roger Summit, President of Dialog, Knight-Ridder indicated that "Dialog will continue as an autonomous activity, and that current operating policies will be continued without disruption." The commitment to high-quality service would be fully supported by Knight-Ridder, according to Summit. Knight-Ridder, known primarily for its newspaper operations, also controls the electronic information source Vu/Text.

ASIS ANNUAL CONFERENCE

The 1988 annual conference of the American Society for Information Science marked the beginning of its 51st year. Its theme, appropriately entitled, was *Information and Technology: Planning*

© 1989 by The Haworth Press, Inc. All rights reserved. *119*

120 COLLECTION MANAGEMENT IN SCI-TECH LIBRARIES

for the Second 50 Years. Although the scope of the papers and panels was wide, ranging from authority files to copyright problems, the dominant topic of many sessions was some aspect of online databases and CD-ROM. Applications of databases to different disciplines, such as art, social sciences and medicine, were plentiful. Both hypertext and hypermedia were featured in special sessions. Two plenary sessions dealt respectively with the role of media and new developments in communications, each session drawing favorable comments from attendees. Attendance was expected to reach 1,000 by the end of the conference.

ONLINE '88

New York City in October 1988 was the scene of ONLINE '88, which celebrated its tenth anniversary. The growth in the conference was evident by a comparison with the first meeting in 1979, when there were 25 exhibitors and 1,150 participants; this year there were approximately 100 exhibitors and attendance was at or over the 2,000 mark.

Like its first meeting, this one featured many papers and discussions on database searching and features of numerous online products. Unlike that meeting, however, this one paid a great deal of attention to CD-ROMs, unknown in 1979. A special room was set aside for 10 exhibitors who could discuss and demonstrate their laserdisk products with interested attendees in quiet surroundings, a plan that met with general approval.

Another new feature was an effort to give special attention to end-users. A 3-hour session allowed end-users to pose questions about searching to a panel of experts, which also discussed common pitfalls of online searching. The session included a discussion of the copyright problem and how it affected downloading on databases.

A session on management decision making covered academic and corporate sectors. One speaker noted that 48% of the incoming freshman class at Indiana University owned their own personal computers, a clear indication that traditional methods of handling information were no longer sufficient for modern times. Competing information services in the corporate and academic worlds were seen as a common problem in both circles.

Discussions on the features of software packages for library use were well-attended, in view of the large quantity of products from which to select.

DATABASE NEWS

Computer ASAP, a full-text database from Information Access Company (IAC) has been added to DIALOG as File 675. The database provides wide-ranging information on computers, electronics and telecommunications. Coverage includes information about the industry, products, companies and people, and technical information about programming, systems management, and computer design. The file contains the complete text and indexing for 70 percent of the articles now indexed in another DIALOG file, *Computer Database* (File 275).

Computer ASAP was designed to answer the questions of business and computer professionals about hardware, software, peripherals, and services, and to provide information regarding high-tech fields such as CD-ROM, desktop publishing, satellite communications, cable television and videotext. Electronic systems and applications, instrumentation, and measurement are also featured. The database includes rigorous product evaluations, comparisons, and best buys, as well as information on the financial stability of computer corporations.

Currently, forty-six of the most widely circulated English-language journals and magazines on computers, electronics and telecommunications are indexed. IAC plans to add the full text of other relevant journals. The bibliographic record contains more than twenty searchable fields, permitting searching on such specific parameters as programming language, operating systems, named persons, product names, company names, and Standard Industrial Classification codes.

Computer ASAP began with approximately 50,000 records. The file is updated monthly with 3,500 records added. IAC expects to update weekly in the future. The price for searching the file is $108 per hour. Printing costs are $2 per full record printed online, and $2.50 for each record printed offline.

122 COLLECTION MANAGEMENT IN SCI-TECH LIBRARIES

SEDBASE Introduced

A new full-text database covering the side effects of drugs is now available via Dialog. *SEDBASE* presents critical analyses of the published drug side-effect literature for drugs currently in use. It includes details of clinically relevant reactions and interactions as reported in the international literature. The database is organized by drug class "chapters" and excludes speculative or unsubstantiated statements.

The file is produced by Elsevier Science Publishers, producers of *EMBASE*. Data for the file are derived from *Meyler's Side Effects of Drugs* and the *Side Effects of Drugs Annuals*. Synonyms for drugs are added to SEDBASE records from Marler's *Pharmacological and Chemical Synonyms*. The Meyler's texts review approximately 9,000 articles on adverse drug reactions each year, published in more than 4,500 journals from over 100 countries.

Drugs in *SEDBASE* can be searched by name, class code, and synonym. In turn, the drug names can be searched in combination with the side effect or interaction name, code, or synonym for effect. Because multiple side effects may be attributed to a given drug, a separate record is generated for every combination of any drug and effect.

SEDBASE records contain full bibliographic citations to the original journal articles, with abstracts included for about fifty percent of the references. Cited references can be searched by title, abstract, journal name, editor, publisher, and publication year. The database contains approximately 25,000 records from the current editions of the printed equivalents. The file will be reloaded quarterly. The price for searching *SEDBASE* (File 70) is $1.35 per minute ($81 per hour). Online or offline print charges are $3.50 per full citation.

SEARCH SYSTEM NEWS

After Dark Unlimited Announced

BRS is now offering access to selected databases at a fixed fee, via After Dark Unlimited. Based on their After Dark service, the new program provides a fixed fee, menu-driven unlimited searching package. The service is designed to provide access to several important databases at a known, fixed cost. Databases included in After Dark Unlimited are: *MEDLINE, ERIC, Magazine Index, INSPEC, AGRICOLA, National Technical Information Service,* and *PsycINFO.* Libraries can purchase multiple copies of the telecommunications software and lend them to patrons without revealing the passwords. The cost of a six-month contract is $13,500. Additional passwords are available at the rate of $2,000 each to a maximum of three. All charges are included; there are no connect time, telecommunications or document charges. For further information contact BRS.

PUBLICATIONS AND SEARCH AIDS

GEOREF Publication Announced

The 1988 edition of the *GEOREF Serials List and KWOC Index* is available. It includes more than 10,000 earth-science serials that have been cited in the database since 1967. *The Serials List* provides the complete title, abbreviated title, CODEN, ISSN, and country of publication for each entry. The *KWOC* (*Key Word Out of Context*) enables the user to identify a serial by any significant word in the title. The publication is available in hard copy for $95; in microfiche for $35. To order it, contact: American Geological Institute, Customer Service Department, 4220 King Street, Alexandria, VA 22302. Telephone: (800) 336-4764 or (703) 379-2480.

New Engineering Search Aid

The Royal Society of Chemistry has announced the availability of the *Chemical Engineering Abstracts User Aid Manual,* for use with the *Chemical Engineering Abstracts* database. The manual includes a detailed description of the contents of the file, controlled vocabulary terms, search hints, and sample searches. The search aid can be ordered, for $20, from the Royal Society of Chemistry, Sales and Promotion Department, The University, Nottingham NG7 2RD, England.

124 COLLECTION MANAGEMENT IN SCI-TECH LIBRARIES

MEDLINE Search Tools

The following 1989 MeSH (Medical Subject Headings) tools may now be ordered from the National Technical Information Service (NTIS) for immediate delivery.

Medical Subject Headings – Annotated Alphabetic List. 1989 PB89-100010/GBB; $28.50 U.S. and Canada ($57 foreign); microfiche $14.50 ($29 foreign).

Medical Subject Headings – Tree Structures, 1989 PB89-100028/GBB; $23 U.S. and Canada ($46 foreign); microfiche $6.95 ($13.90 foreign).

Permuted Medical Subject Headings, 1989 PB89-100036/GBB; $23 U.S. and Canada ($46 foreign); microfiche $6.95 ($13.90 foreign).

Orders should be sent to: National Technical Information Service, U.S. Department of Commerce, 5285 Port Royal Road, Springfield, VA 22161. Phone orders will be accepted from individuals with an NTIS deposit account or major credit card. Telephone: (703) 487-4650. Remittance should be sent with all mail orders. There is a $3 shipping/handling charge, per order.

EDUCATION

AGRICOLA Training Program

The National Agricultural Library is conducting basic and advanced courses on the *AGRICOLA* database, designed for searchers who want to utilize the files more efficiently. Workshops provide an equal amount of time for classroom lectures and hands-on practice.

The Basic *AGRICOLA* Workshop, is a three-day course, and includes basic instruction in online searching, the essentials of the database, and information on other agriculturally related databases. The Advanced Workshop, a one-day course, offers an in-depth look at subject, chronological, geographic and source access to the database.

There is a registration fee of $150 for the Basic Workshop and

$50 for the Advanced course. The fee covers online searching practice time and instructional materials. For a copy of the registration form and additional information contact *AGRICOLA* Training, National Agricultural Library, Special Services Branch, Room 1402, Beltsville, MD 20705; telephone: (301) 344-3875.

LETTER TO THE EDITOR

I enjoyed the article by Sarah Thomas Kadec and Carol B. Watts on the history of Federal scientific libraries in Volume 8, Number 1 of *Science & Technology Libraries*, "One Hundred Years of Sci-Tech Libraries: A Brief History." To make the record more complete for the period between 1901 and 1941, I'd like to provide some information about the two Federal sci-tech libraries I've been associated with during my library career.

In 1927, the Naval Research Laboratory (NRL), widely recognized as one of this country's major scientific research institutions, established its Library. NRL had been created in 1923 as a result of a recommendation made by Thomas A. Edison for a government research facility. Its library, renamed in 1975 the Ruth H. Hooker Technical Library after the first NRL Librarian, has for its 61-year history supported the scientific and technical efforts of the Navy with a major research collection emphasizing physics and chemistry.

The other library, which came into being during that period, was that of the Coast and Geodetic Survey (now the National Ocean Service, part of the National Oceanic and Atmospheric Administration, NOAA). If I recall correctly, the Survey was established about 1907 and the library sometime later, about 1920. The other major historical component of NOAA's extensive collection dates from about 1890, when the Weather Bureau (now the National Weather Service) established its library. As Ms. Watts is now director of the NOAA library in Rockville, MD, she could probably expand further on these developments.

Laurie E. Stackpole, Chief Librarian
Ruth H. Hooker Technical Library
Naval Research Laboratory
Washington, DC 20375-5000

© 1989 by The Haworth Press, Inc. All rights reserved.

Milton Keynes UK
Ingram Content Group UK Ltd.
UKHW050719210624
444299UK00007B/18